The Lion, the Mouse and the Dawn Treader

SPIRITUAL LESSONS FROM C. S. LEWIS'S NARNIA

Carl McColman

PARACLETE PRESS

BREWSTER, MASSACHUSETTS

The Lion, the Mouse and the Dawn Treader: Spiritual Lessons from C. S. Lewis's Narnia

2011   First Printing

Copyright © 2011 by Carl McColman

ISBN: 978-1-55725-887-8

Scripture quotations are from the New Revised Standard Version Bible, © 1989, Division of Christian Education of the National Council of Churches of Christ in the United States of America. Used by permission. All rights reserved.

McColman, Carl.
  The lion, the mouse, and the Dawn Treader : spiritual lessons from C.S. Lewis's Narnia / Carl McColman.
    p. cm.
  Includes bibliographical references.
  ISBN 978-1-55725-887-8
  1. Lewis, C. S. (Clive Staples), 1898-1963. Voyage of the Dawn Treader. 2. Lewis, C. S. (Clive Staples), 1898-1963. Chronicles of Narnia. 3. Christian fiction, English--History and criticism. 4. Spiritual life in literature. I. Title.
  PR6023.E926V6936 2010
  823'.912--dc22

                        2010041987

10 9 8 7 6 5 4 3 2 1

Published by Paraclete Press
Brewster, Massachusetts
www.paracletepress.com
Printed in the United States of America

For all who love Narnia,
AND ESPECIALLY THOSE WHO SEEK THE RADIANT LIGHT OF THE SILVER SEA
—AND BEYOND.

Contents

Invitation to an Adventure

JESUS TOLD his followers, "[W]hoever does not receive the kingdom of God as a little child will never enter it" (Mark 10:15). To put a more positive spin on this challenging statement, we who seek to live a Christlike life will do well to embrace the heart and mind of a child as part of our spiritual practice.

This is easier said than done. In our frantic and hyperpaced world, many of us are doing the best we can to make sure we get the bills paid and the dishes done. We barely have time to get a full night's sleep; how can we afford to entertain the question of "entering the kingdom of heaven," let alone try to figure out what it means to receive heaven "as a little child"?

I believe Jesus was trying to get his followers (and that includes you and me) to shut off the overly rational, excessively analytical mind, not in the interest of some sort of naïve denial, but rather in recognition that openness and even playfulness are helpful qualities whenever we try to learn or understand something new. When we adopt such a childlike perspective, we open ourselves to listen for the still, small voice of God and see the hidden actions of the Holy Spirit in the midst of the ordinary miracles that occur every day (but that we are usually too busy to notice).

How, then, do we become "as a little child"? I certainly do not have all the answers. But one idea I do have is that we can seek the heart and mind of a child by doing some childlike things. And one of those things, which is the subject of this book, is to read a children's novel—hopefully giving ourselves permission to read it *like a child*, which is to say, playfully and without being too critical or quick to judge.

This is tricky, and here is an example. The book I have chosen to explore with you is *The Voyage of the Dawn Treader,* one of the beloved Chronicles of Narnia by C. S. Lewis. The Narnia series consists of seven novels, written for children (of all ages), and each one offering insight into a different dimension of the Christian faith. As wonderful as these stories are, they were written in the 1950s, and sometimes they show their age. *The Voyage of the Dawn Treader* begins by making fun of people who do not drink or smoke or eat meat. Well, I am a nonsmoking vegetarian who doesn't drink very much, so immediately my grown-up mind wants to argue with the author. Not a very auspicious beginning! So I have to remind myself that C. S. Lewis, writing more than a half century ago, held an entirely different set of values about dietary and health practices than I do, or perhaps than most people do, today. And then I have to forget about it, in the interest of reading this book like a child.

I'd like to invite you to forget about all your adult tendencies to rush to judgment. Take Jesus at his word: "Do not judge" (Matthew 7:1), and simply enter into this charming tale about a magical sea voyage in a mystical land called Narnia. Maybe you are like me and you have been reading and rereading the Narnia books ever since you were as young as its main characters. Or, perhaps, you are new to these tales, having just stumbled across them recently. Either way, I invite you simply to be present with the tale, and to let it unfold.

C. S. Lewis has made no secret that these stories are filled with Christian themes and metaphors. Several of the Narnia tales feature plotlines that echo events in the Bible:

+ *The Magician's Nephew* explores the themes of creation and the origin of evil, originally found in the book of Genesis.
+ *The Lion, the Witch and the Wardrobe* offers insight into the Gospel story of the passion, death, and resurrection of Jesus (through the Christlike figure of Aslan, the noble Lion).

✦ And *The Last Battle* looks toward the end of time and the hope of eternal life, similar to themes in the last book of the New Testament, the Revelation to John.

By contrast, *The Voyage of the Dawn Treader* is not directly related to any stories in the Bible. Even so, it may be the most useful of the seven Narnia books, for it is the one that most directly maps out the contours of the Christian spiritual life.

Since the earliest centuries of the Christian era, mystics and saints have described the spirituality of Christian living in the language of *journey*. Christians are, according to the greatest exemplars of the spiritual life, walking along the way of the pilgrim: we are ascending Mount Carmel, climbing the stairway of perfection, or scaling the ladder of divine ascent. In a more abstract way, mystics have described the life in Christ by talking about successive stages—such as *purgation*, letting go of everything that holds us back from God; to *illumination*, moving more deeply into God's radiant presence; and finally, *union*, arriving at that most mysterious of places, where we truly realize that "in him we live and move and have our being" (Acts 17:28).

Likewise, one of the greatest literary traditions in the Christian world, the story of the quest for the Holy Grail, serves as an allegory of the Christian life. So the mystical dimension of following Jesus can be understood both as a journey and a quest. This is the foundation on which C. S. Lewis built the story of the *Dawn Treader*.

If you are not familiar with the Chronicles of Narnia, you are in for a treat, and I suspect that if you read just one of these books, you'll want to read all seven. Taken as a whole, the Narnia series tells the story of a number of English children who, over about a sixty- to seventy-year period, discover various portals through which they can move into an alternate reality: a land of magical talking animals and sometimes frightening confrontations between forces of good and evil. Narnia is ruled by the good and noble Lion, Aslan, who comes "from over the water." Aslan represents Christ, and is the true hero of the Narnia Chronicles, more so than the children who voyage from our world to his.

Along with the three Narnia tales that have clear connections to Biblical events, four other novels consider other dimensions of faith.

+ *Prince Caspian* examines the need to be faithful, even when it is not popular or safe to do so.
+ *The Silver Chair* considers the importance of perseverance and mindfulness—paying attention to the "signs" we have been given of Divine guidance.
+ *The Horse and His Boy* explores the psychology of conversion—of longing for the sacred mystery that

Christians call God, and finding one's true home in the heart of the Divine.

✦ And finally, *The Voyage of the Dawn Treader* is the novel where, instead of instructing his readers in biblical truth, C. S. Lewis navigates another important dimension of the Christian faith: the stormy seas and calm waters that reveal the nature of the lifelong spiritual journey.

Of course, this needs to be understood as a metaphor. The *Dawn Treader* makes for a great story, but in reality we are not all sailors, navigating through uncharted seas in search of lost people or hoping to find heaven on earth. But we do all "sail" over the deep waters of our individual lives. Sometimes these waters are peaceful and quiet, and at other times they are dynamic and dangerous. We visit many "islands" over the course of our lives: the lands of childhood, of education, of romance and marriage, of career, of parenting, and eventually of retirement and old age. As earthly Christians, we seek the guidance of "Aslan" as we know him—Jesus, the Son of God. Sometimes he seems very close, and at other times quite far away.

So let's turn to *The Voyage of the Dawn Treader* and see how this charming children's tale has, encoded in it, much of the wisdom and insight about spiritual living that has come down to us over the centuries from the great mystics and saints of the Christian world. It's a great adventure story on its own terms. But when understood as a metaphor for the mystical life, *Dawn Treader* becomes even more wonderful. It's wonderful because it can help ordinary folks like you and me to recognize, understand, and appreciate all the many aspects of the spiritual journey. Like all adventure stories, *The Voyage of the Dawn Treader* features good guys and villains, challenges and trials, moments of suspense and times of serene wonder and quiet joy. But what sets this story apart from so many others is this recurring theme: at the heart of the journey, but also at its destination, resides a great, glorious, and personal Presence, who guides and loves all who seek him. It is this very Presence who gives the sublime moments of the adventure their beauty, and who also gives all the trials and challenges their meaning. When you and I explore the *Dawn Treader* and its voyage to the end of the world (and beyond), we are invited to seek after this Presence in our own lives. In other words, we are invited to embark on our own unique adventure.

So what are we waiting for? Let's go!

The Land of the Lion

BEFORE WE DIVE into *The Voyage of the Dawn Treader*, let's take a look at the realm of Narnia—the magical otherworld created by C. S. Lewis as the backdrop to the story of Aslan, the awe-inspiring Lion.

If you are not familiar with the concept of an "otherworld," it comes from Celtic mythology—the mythology of lands such as Wales and Ireland (C. S. Lewis was born and grew up in Belfast). The ancient Celts were very spiritual, as their myths and legends attest. They believed that intimately connected to the "real" or visible world were magical realms where gods, goddesses, fairies, and even the spirits of the ancestors live. The otherworld might exist parallel to the physical world, or perhaps underneath it (the "underworld"), or even just somewhere beyond the ocean. Much Celtic lore concerned stories of mortal human beings who encountered the inhabitants of the otherworld, sometimes even traveling to this mysterious alternate universe by various means.

In our time, this concept of an alternate universe—an otherworld—is a recurring motif in children's literature. Harry Potter travels to a school for witches and wizards via a magical train; Alice finds her Wonderland by falling down a rabbit hole; and Peter Pan lures the Darling children to Neverland by helping them to fly (with the aid of a little bit of pixie dust). The children in these adventure stories often find that their journey to the otherworld involves some sort of quest or challenge. By completing the quest and overcoming the obstacles along the way, they learn lessons and develop skills that will aid them even after they return to the mundane world.

The heroes and heroines of the Narnia Chronicles have their own quests. Whenever any of them travel from their ordinary lives as children in England to the magical realm of Narnia, a task or a challenge of some sort awaits them. Some of the children embrace their quest, while others seem to do everything they can to avoid their calling. Regardless of whether they accept or resist the purpose for being in Narnia, one thing is for sure: they are all changed by their experience there.

What truly sets Narnia apart from most other alternate worlds is the explicit Christian character of the land, and especially of its supreme being, Aslan. Although C. S. Lewis insisted that the Narnia Chronicles are not allegories, they all contain a clear spiritual message. Lewis knew that children love a good story, and that sometimes the best way to understand a principle or an idea might be to see it enacted in a fictional or a mythical setting. So, even though the Narnia Chronicles are so well crafted that everyone (including people who have no interest in religion or spirituality) can enjoy them, for those of us who do choose to discern the hidden (mystical) meaning of the stories, they come alive with rich layers of insight—into God, into human nature, and into the dynamics of how God relates to us mere mortals.

An important part of any mythical otherworld is its quality of magic and wonder. C. S. Lewis weaves a sense of wonder into Narnia in three ways: first, by endowing many of the animals of Narnia with the gift of speech. Second, he populates Narnia with exotic and unusual beings such as fauns, centaurs, and minotaurs—characters who have their roots in earthly myth and legend, but who come vividly to life under the genius of the author's pen. In *The Voyage of the Dawn Treader*, for example, mermaids, dragons, sea serpents, and even a fallen star appear at various stages along the journey. But the third source of wonder in these tales is by far the most important, and this is Aslan himself. Described as the "Son of the Emperor-Over-the-Sea," Aslan is the true and compassionate ruler of the land; he is loving and kind but uncompromising in his commitment to goodness, justice, and virtue. The children who serve as the heroes and heroines of Narnia—such as Lucy, Edmund, and Eustace—all have profound and life-changing encounters with Aslan.

Narnia is itself a beautiful land, filled with majestic forests, rolling rivers, mountains, marshes, plains, and deserts. Lewis, like his friend J. R. R. Tolkien, created a mythic world rich with bucolic splendor. If you read all seven of the Narnia Chronicles, you will learn of the entire history of this land, from when it was literally sung into existence by Aslan, through successive ages of kingdoms and conflicts (several of which are decisively aided by earthly children), to its last days, marked by an apocalyptic conflict with a glorious resolution. From the great forests of the west, the land of Narnia stretches to a coastline on the east, where—of particular importance to the *Dawn Treader*—a sea stretches out beyond the Narnian shore, all the way to the very end of the world, where the sun rises. Beyond this sea, and beyond the very end of the world, lies Aslan's country, where he resides, along with his mysterious father.

Like earth, Narnia suffers from the existence of evil, seen in characters with names like Jadis or Shift, who oppose Aslan in several of the chronicles. Interestingly, though, *The Voyage of the Dawn Treader*, while featuring a few minor bad guys like Gumpas and Pug, does not revolve around an epic tale of good versus evil. Rather, most of the conflict explored on the *Dawn Treader* is the kind that each and every one of us faces—within ourselves.

One interesting quality of Narnia is that time progresses there with no correlation to the passage of time on our earth. So a child can slip away into Narnia, stay an afternoon—or a decade—and return to find that barely a second has elapsed here in our world. Likewise, a year passing in our world might correspond to centuries or even a millennium of Narnian time. In fact, the entire history of Narnia, from creation to the end of Narnian time, takes place within a single lifetime in our world (that of Digory Kirke, who is one of the more important characters in the Chronicles as a whole but who does not appear in *The Voyage of the Dawn Treader*).

No character, aside from Aslan, appears in all the Narnian stories. Aslan himself seems rather unpredictable, coming and going as he pleases, playing a significant role in some stories but being seemingly almost absent altogether from others. He does appear rather frequently in the *Dawn Treader* adventure, but often to just one or a few characters at a time, and then only briefly. But whenever he does appear, something significant happens.

The otherworld of Narnia is, as C. S. Lewis insisted, not meant to be seen as an allegory for our world, where each element of Narnia symbolizes something about earthly existence. Rather, the magic, the fauns, the talking beasts, and the sylvan splendor of Narnia are simply enjoyable elements of a rollicking good adventure story (or, rather a suite of stories), providing a mythical setting where the various characters can discover the lessons and principles of spirituality—of encountering and relating to the Great Lion himself. Hopefully, the boys and girls who come to Narnia from England will take these lessons and principles to heart, and thereby lead renewed and transformed lives once they return home. Meanwhile, we who read the Narnian books (and watch the motion picture adaptations of them) may likewise be renewed and transformed by the insights we glean from Aslan and his dealings with the boys and girls of our world. We might only hope to visit an otherworld like Narnia in our dreams—but we can still reap the benefits of this otherworld, whenever we take from these stories insights and ideas that can nurture our spiritual lives, here in the "real" world.

So, now, let's turn our attention specifically to the most mystical of the seven Narnia Chronicles: *The Voyage of the Dawn Treader.*

The Journey Begins

VERY STORY has a beginning, a middle, and an end. It's more than just a platitude that your seventh-grade English teacher told you: it's true of your "story," your life adventure, as well. Christianity, likewise, places great emphasis on the beginning of things. The biblical books of Genesis and the Gospel of John stress how God is engaged in the act of creation, from the very first moment of time. And God is intimately present in your and my "beginnings" as well: he is always calling to us, beckoning to us to take that first, all-important step on the adventure of spirituality. As we will see in *The Voyage of the Dawn Treader,* sometimes the call to begin a spiritual adventure comes even when we least expect it.

Speaking of beginnings, it's a good thing I first read *The Voyage of the Dawn Treader* when I was a youth. Otherwise, the second time I read it (at age twenty-six), I might not have made it past the very first page.

C. S. Lewis begins this story by zeroing in on Eustace
Clarence Scrubb, a scientifically minded youngster who
seems to be part nerd and part bully. To explain how this
boy got to be so awful, the author notes that his parents were
vegetarians and didn't drink or smoke. Maybe in 1952 this
worked as a type of humor, but in 1987 (let alone today)
it just seemed to fall flat. Being a vegetarian myself, I had
to fight the temptation to feel insulted by Lewis's heavy-
handed attempt at a joke.

Thankfully, I'm more forgiving nowadays than I was in my
twenties. I realize that Lewis was simply poking fun at the
kind of person who believes that, by managing their own
health and maximizing their "human potential," they don't
need God and certainly can't be bothered with religion. I've
come to realize that some vegetarians can be as irritating
about their diet as some Christians are about their faith.
"Have you been born again?" and "Do you realize what
meat does to your arteries?" are, in polite conversation,
functionally equivalent in their certainty to do little more
than annoy the person to whom the question, always in an
accusing tone, is posed.

So I'm willing to decide that Alberta and Harold Scrubb
were not just teetotaling nonsmoking herbivores, but they
were militant about it all. And they passed on to their
son, Eustace, who turns out to be one of most important
characters in this adventure, their smug sense of pride

at how well managed their life seems to be. For this is, ultimately, what the Scrubbs are all about: pride.

Eustace has two cousins, Edmund and Lucy, who appeared in two previous Narnia adventures, *The Lion, the Witch and the Wardrobe* and *Prince Caspian*. The cousins are visiting him while their parents and older siblings are otherwise occupied, and no one seems particularly happy about this arrangement. Eustace taunts his cousins and takes every opportunity to boss them around; they, meanwhile, struggle to maintain a basic sense of civility in his presence.

One day Lucy admires a painting of a ship in her bedroom, and she and Edmund remark about how it reminds them of a Narnian sailing ship. Overhearing them, Eustace (who thinks they are playing a game) teases them, but before their interaction can escalate into an all-out fight, the painting magically comes alive. Suddenly, the three children find themselves plunged into the ocean of Narnia, where the ship—the *Dawn Treader*—comes to their rescue. Edmund and Lucy are thrilled to suddenly find themselves back in this land of wonders and delight, while Eustace, shocked and upset at how his life has suddenly spun beyond what he could easily control, reacts with anger and vitriol.

◦⤙⤚◦

Notice how the three children do not themselves choose to visit Narnia. Granted, Lucy and Edmund would have gladly accepted any invitation to return to Aslan's world, but that is just to say that they were *disposed* to going. They were on call, so to speak; ready, willing, and able to leave our world behind for the adventure of Narnia. But they were also resigned, if not happily, to the fact that they themselves could not choose when to enter Narnia. Their willingness was, in essence, a gift to Aslan (the majestic Lion who is the lord of Narnia), without any expectation or sense of entitlement in return. They wanted to make the journey, but knew that all they could do was *respond* to a call—if it ever came.

Eustace stands in a different place, however. Smugly arrogant and used to thinking about life in terms of the dynamics of dominance and submission, he dismisses Narnia (like all spiritual talk) as only so much hogwash, and believes that this magical land is nothing more than a product of his cousins' overactive imagination. Even if he could be persuaded that Narnia *were* real, he'd have no desire or intention to visit the place. For Eustace, only that which can be turned to his advantage has any merit or value. Nothing has any value in itself; everything has worth only insofar as it can be used or exploited. A magical land filled with talking creatures and governed by codes of chivalry and traditional ethics and morality? Eustace would probably say that such a place sounds, at best, unimaginably dull.

Nevertheless, Eustace is summoned to Narnia right alongside Lucy and Edmund. Stunned and infuriated by this turn of events, his desire to keep the circumstances of his life under tight control are, as it turns out, utterly useless to protect him from Narnia's call. Here, then, is our first lesson about the spiritual journey: we enter it not merely by virtue of our own desire, but always at the pleasure of God.

In other words, whether or not we *want* a spiritual adventure ultimately makes no difference. Incidentally, I'm using words like *spirituality* and *mysticism* more or less interchangeably, but they do have different meanings. Spirituality refers to the dimension of living intentionally in relationship with God, whereas mysticism implies a can't-miss-it experience of God's presence in our lives, even to the point of feeling at one with God. Evelyn Underhill, a renowned Christian writer, called it "a life based on . . . conscious communion with God."[1] Another theologian, Karl Rahner, once famously said, "the Christian of the future will be a mystic or will not exist at all."[2] This suggests that, at least as far as Christians are concerned, spirituality (relating to God) sooner or later will include a dimension of mysticism (experiencing God's presence). But that may take many different forms. Even some of the holiest Christians

---

1 Evelyn Underhill, *Mystics of the Church* (Cambridge, UK: James Clarke & Co. Ltd., 1925), 10.
2 Karl Rahner, *Concern for the Church* (New York: Crossroad, 1981), 149.

(for example, Mother Teresa of Calcutta) often are more aware of God's seeming *absence* than God's felt *presence*.

It seems that many people who desperately want mystical experience never receive it—or, perhaps better said, never seem to receive the call in precisely the way they would *like* to receive it—while others who have no interest in spirituality or mysticism whatsoever might find their lives suddenly shattered wide open by the intrusion of the numinous in their lives ("numinous" is another word that refers to the experience of the presence of God).

Certainly it is a good thing to desire such numinous, mystical blessings, for being so disposed enables us to receive God's gifts with joy, in whatever way or at whatever moment they may be granted to us. But having such a desire cannot guarantee if, or when, or how, we will receive such an extraordinary, transformational blessing—just as having no interest in spirituality cannot guarantee that we will be untouched by its impact. This first lesson about the mystical life teaches us an important, foundational truth: mysticism is always God's call, and our experience (or non-experience) of God remains always and entirely at his pleasure.

If this kind of thinking makes you bristle, I hope you will try to make your peace with it now. For this theme of "God's in charge and you're not" will recur again and again throughout the *Dawn Treader*'s journey.

TWO

The Point of Departure

S. LEWIS DID NOT consider himself a mystic. In one of his final books, *Letters to Malcolm*, he describes a mystic as someone who scales the high mountains of prayer, whereas Lewis presents himself as someone who never makes it beyond the foothills. I think he was being humble, but he also was operating with a narrow definition of "mystic" as someone who has truly extraordinary and even supernatural experiences of God's presence. Other respected Christian thinkers, such as Evelyn Underhill or Karl Rahner, saw mysticism in a much broader and inclusive way—involving not so much a *supernatural* relationship with God, but simply an *experiential* one. In this sense, not only was Lewis no doubt more of a mystic than he gave himself credit for but indeed, Karl Rahner was right: *all* Christians are called to the mystical life.

While Lewis may not have considered himself a mystic, he certainly was interested in mysticism, as David C. Downing demonstrates in his book *Into the Region of Awe: Mysticism in C. S. Lewis*. Downing writes, "Given his habit of grappling with theological issues both critically and creatively, it is not surprising that Lewis's interest in mysticism, mentioned so often in his essays and letters, should find imaginative expression in the Narnia Chronicles."[3] And while mystical elements may be found in all seven of the Narnia books, none describe the mystical life as fully as *The Voyage of the Dawn Treader*.

In *Letters to Malcolm*, Lewis refutes the idea that mystical experiences are an end in themselves. As he saw it, mysticism, by itself, is neither good nor evil; it is the content or the object of mystical experience that determines its ultimate value. "Departures are all alike; it is the landfall that crowns the voyage."[4] In other words, any kind of mystical experience is simply a "departure" from normal awareness and ordinary reality. It's like seeing a glorious site in nature—the Grand Canyon, for example—for the first time. The beauty, the vastness, the austerity—these all combine to create an experience of wonder, or of humility, or even of ecstasy. Or, think of how some people's lives are

---

3 David C. Downing, *Into the Region of Awe* (Downers Grove: InterVarsity Press, 2005), 127.

4 C. S. Lewis, *Letters to Malcolm: Chiefly on Prayer* (San Diego: Harcourt, 1963), 65.

changed when they encounter suffering, or poverty, or other forms of human need. The experience of compassion and sadness in the face of human misery can change a person's life forever (here, again, Mother Teresa is a great example). But an experience, in itself, does not make someone a mystic. Whether an experience is one of great joy, or love, or sorrow, or suffering, or even a more "classic" mystical experience of feeling God's presence in our hearts, we need to ask: where does this experience take us? Lewis goes on to say, "The saint, by being a saint, proves that his mysticism (if he was a mystic; not all saints are) led him aright; the fact that he has practiced mysticism could never prove his sanctity."[5] In other words, mysticism does not necessarily make a person a saint, nor does sanctity necessarily make one a mystic. For Lewis, there's no contest: if we have to choose between being a spiritual master and a holy person, seek holiness. Better to be humble and holy than to be mystical and lost in the illusions of our own egos.

This principle underlies the action in the early chapters of *The Voyage of the Dawn Treader*. The first half of the book is very much Eustace's story—and at first Eustace is, frankly, not a very likable character. He is lazy, arrogant, whiny, quick to criticize but slow to lend a hand. And, as one might expect from a person with his character (or lack thereof), he is utterly oblivious to how others perceive him. He is so

5 Ibid, 65.

busy contemptuously finding fault with everyone else that he never bothers to look into a mirror and truly consider his own foibles. Humility, compassion, and kindness are words that seem to be utterly absent from Eustace's vocabulary.

Given his almost cartoonish flaws, one might wonder why, when Lucy and Edmund were summoned back to Narnia, Eustace was summoned as well. After all, just minutes before the three children are spirited away to the *Dawn Treader*, Lucy and Edmund were alone with the magical painting. As troublesome—and unhappy—as Eustace turns out to be, wouldn't it have made much more sense all the way around if he had been left back in England while his cousins made their adventure without him?

Of course, the answer to this question echoes the principle we considered in chapter one: that mysticism is ultimately God's action, and God can call whomever he chooses—even a thoroughly "undeserving" character like Eustace. But just because God calls someone to the spiritual life does not obviously make that person "holy" or "mystical." As Lewis so clearly understood, mysticism (or spirituality in general), by itself, does not make a saint out of a sinner.

Indeed, when Edmund and Lucy (with their older brother and sister) first ventured to Narnia (a tale told in *The Lion, the Witch and the Wardrobe*), Edmund was, if anything, even worse than Eustace, and his actions had far graver consequences. But just as Edmund found a change of heart in Narnia, so, eventually will Eustace. Their transformations, however, came about not because of where they were, but rather simply because of the choices they made. It is conceivable that Edmund and Eustace could have gone to Narnia and never experienced a change of heart; likewise, they could have had such a conversion experience even if they had never visited Narnia at all. It is our choices that matter, even more than what spiritual or mystical experiences we do (or don't) have.

Why is it that some people have powerful, life-altering experiences of God, while others never do? It seems not to matter whether one is a believer or not. Perhaps the most famous conversion story in Christian history is that of St. Paul, who had set off on a journey to persecute Christians when he experienced a mystical vision of Jesus. This vision left him temporary blinded and dependent on the kindness of strangers—in fact, of Christian strangers (this is all the more dramatic since Paul was famous for his persecution of Christians, and indeed could have had his benefactors arrested). But following his mystical encounter with Jesus, Paul had been transformed. He gave up his former life and became a great leader of the New Testament church.

The kind of dramatic, earth-shaking event that Paul experienced is, at best, extremely rare. The vast majority of Christians are humble believers who never experience anything "supernatural"—but rather go through their entire lives with little more than their faith and the support of their church to guide their spiritual lives.

It is a mystery why this is so. We can assume that when it comes to mysticism, God knows what is best, and while some people do seem to experience extraordinary, miraculous encounters with the Ultimate Mystery, most others have a much more down-to-earth spirituality. It is wise not to compare ourselves with others, and to trust that each of us is given the type of spirituality (and experience) that is best for us. It's also important to bear in mind that a sweet experience of God does not make us holy, or sanctified, or better than others. True holiness, in fact, is related to humility, which often leads us to be painfully aware of how *flawed* we are, not how "good" we are. Holiness requires not experience, but faith, commitment, a change of heart, and a willingness to let God remake us according to his design.

THREE

The Captivity of Sin

NE OF THE MISSIONS of the *Dawn Treader* is to find seven missing lords from Narnia, who sailed into exile during the reign of Miraz the Usurper. Now that Caspian is the rightful king of Narnia, he has embarked on this voyage to find the seven noblemen, or at least learn of their fate. The first stop on this journey is the Lone Islands, where one of the lords will be found—but in the midst of a most unpleasant adventure.

A landing party consisting of King Caspian, Edmund, Lucy, Eustace, and Reepicheep the Mouse disembark onto the apparently uninhabited island of Felimath, while the *Dawn Treader* sails around it. But before they can rendezvous with the ship on the other side of the island, the landing party runs into a group of men who turn out to be slave traders—who promptly kidnap them. Thankfully, a landowner comes by and purchases Caspian from the slavers; he turns out to be Lord Bern, the first of the missing Narnian lords. After he and Caspian reveal their identity to one another, they begin to plot how to rescue the rest of the captured party.

With this unhappy turn of events, C. S. Lewis turns his attention to one of the most important topics for anyone who is serious about the Christian life—and yet, a topic that is singularly unpopular in our time. What I am referring to, of course, is sin. In *The Voyage of the Dawn Treader*, Lewis uses three dramatic metaphors for sin:

- ✦ being sold into slavery;
- ✦ being turned into a dragon;
- ✦ and using magic to gain power over others.

The dragon and magic metaphors both involve questions of individual choice and responsibility, as the occasion of sin involves someone acting alone (Eustace and Lucy, respectively), whereas the slavery metaphor has a social dimension, in which an entire society is involved in the sinful action. I think Lewis was quite wise to present the "slavery" metaphor first.

The concept of sin has become unpopular in our day because previous generations made the mistake of overemphasizing sin as strictly a matter of personal immorality, and underemphasizing the social dimension of sin. When Christians seem to be overly concerned with sexual ethics, but turn a blind eye to such systemic evils as racism or poverty, it is no wonder that society as a whole has become suspicious of the concept of sin. It seems rather hypocritical to guilt-trip people for their individual actions while ignoring what most reasonable people would agree are far more serious matters of injustice, oppression, and abuse.

But if our society has made progress toward addressing systemic ills such as racism or harm to the environment, perhaps we have ironically become too lax in regard to our standards of personal conduct and individual character. Widespread substance abuse, broken families, white collar crime, and materialism (financed by excessive debt) all seem to suggest that there is a price to be paid for ignoring old-fashioned ideas such as virtue, honor, and responsibility. Sin may be out of fashion, but it appears to be very much still with us.

Against both the historical tendency to overemphasize sin as personal immorality, and our current tendency to de-emphasize the same, Lewis provides a balanced view, recognizing that sin has both a social and a personal dimension. First, he looks at the social nature of sin, as symbolized by the slave traders. And look at who gets captured by the slavers: not just "sinful" Eustace, but also Lucy, Edmund, Reepicheep, and Caspian himself. The message is that sin affects everyone, no matter one's disposition, gender, social status, race, or creed. Whether someone seems to be good-natured or evil-tempered makes no difference. Social sin implicates everyone and ultimately wounds everyone.

As Lewis recounts the story of Caspian's company falling prey to slave traders, it could be easy to see this as a simple story about oppressors and their victims. Certainly, a key feature of sin is that it often entails institutionalized forms of oppression and abuse (for example, part of what made racism so pernicious in American society was the existence of Jim Crow laws, by which racism was literally written into the legal code of many states). A lone person who is a racist is simply unpleasant and despicable, and while such a person can be dangerous if violent, the scope of his wrong-doing will be relatively limited. But an entire racist society is capable of horrific, wide-scale evil. As wrong as it is for individuals to be bigoted, the true scope of this, and all, collective sin is only truly revealed in its corporate, social, and institutional forms.

Lewis hints that when Caspian decides to take a landing party to the apparently uninhabited island of Felimath, he is making a bad decision due to his inexperience as an adventurer. In truth, all of those who accompany him do so willingly. The author is not blaming the victim, but he is suggesting that there is folly in carelessly placing oneself in harm's way. We could see this as a way of suggesting that social sin is always complex, and involves not only the evil of the predator, but also the mistakes of the prey. Sin, after all, comes from a Hebrew concept with a meaning like "missing the mark" (as an arrow shot that flies wide of its target)—in other words, a mistake. So, while sin is generally understood in the sense of willful rejection of the will of God (and, therefore, intentionally unloving), a full understanding of sin implies that even innocent choices that enable or unwittingly abet the cause of abuse and oppression ought to be recognized as mistakes in their own right. Someone who neglects to install a security alarm is not guilty of a sin—but when their house is burglarized, they nevertheless pay a price for their carelessness. Social ills such as racism and sexism are not just the problem of people who are racist and sexist—rather, we are *all* obligated to work together to help liberate our world from such scourges.

Whether arising from willful evil or negligent mistakes, sin always undermines love and separates us from God and from one another. But the spiritual life is a journey toward becoming a more truly loving and caring person, both toward God and toward others. Christianity teaches that God has empowered us with the ability to fight against sin and evil, whether this means overcoming temptations to say hurtful things to those we love, or engaging in a more public struggle against such evils as human trafficking or gang violence. In a very real way, Christianity (in its truest, fullest and most authentic expression) always stands against injustice, oppression, abuse, and slavery.

Therefore, the Christian spiritual life necessarily involves struggle against sin in all forms. Hopefully anyone who accepts the call to the adventure of the mystical life will not in any way support racism, sexism, classism, or other forms of oppression. But even sincere followers of Christ will encounter these and other evils in our lives, and will have to address the ways in which we have unwittingly tolerated, or even contributed to, such ills. Every one of us who embarks on the spiritual life will have to come to grips with the fact that sin, in one way or another, has enslaved us all. As Saint Paul sorrowfully noted, "For I do not do the good I want, but the evil I do not want is what I do" (Romans 7:19). If sin causes us to do what we do not want to do, in a very real sense, it has enslaved us.

So before we go any further on our spiritual journey, we need at least to begin to deal with this problem. For you and me, this means finding ways to free ourselves from anything in our lives, big or small, that stands in the way of more fully loving God (and each other). That could be as simple as overcoming a bad habit of swearing, or as life-changing as leaving an abusive relationship. Perhaps we also need to consider how we contribute to larger-scale issues like economic inequality or global warming. None of us can solve all our problems, let alone the world's problems, by ourselves—or overnight. But at this point in the journey, what matters the most is simply getting started.

Standing Up for What Is Right

IKE MANY CHILDREN, when I was young I became very concerned about environmental issues. I knew that the dinosaurs had once roamed the earth but were now extinct, and learned how humankind's impact on the earth's ecosystem resulted in many other species of plants and animals disappearing forever. It didn't take long for my overactive imagination to realize that, at the rate we were going, perhaps one day human beings themselves would be extinct!

It was one thing to learn about environmental issues and develop my own views about what needed to be done. But when, in the sixth grade, I went to a new school where an active Ecology Club provided students ways to become involved in recycling campaigns and even letter-writing to politicians, I found new meaning and purpose in my values. Through the Ecology Club, I learned not only many things about the environment, but also important life lessons: first, that it's not enough just to think the right thoughts, but we must also act according to our convictions; and second, that it's easier to do so when we join together with others who share our values and beliefs.

The previous chapter of *The Voyage of the Dawn Treader* ended with King Caspian having been redeemed from slavery by the good Lord Bern—one of the seven missing Narnian lords. In chapter four, C. S. Lewis recounts Bern's and Caspian's adventures as they confront the negligent governor of the Lone Isles, restore the order of law to the Isles under Narnian standards and authority, and then free the slaves who have been victimized by the criminals who had, until then, operated freely under the corrupt government.

While on the surface none of this may seem very "spiritual"—Lewis appears only to be telling a good adventure story here—this chapter in fact is pointing to an important, if not very glamorous, dimension of the spiritual life: confronting evil wherever it occurs, establishing good order and harmony, and (of course) setting the prisoners free. For most of us this chapter can only be understood in a metaphorical way, but it still conveys an important message. For we are all prisoners of sin, and so a key step on the mystical path is working to spring ourselves—and each other—from our symbolic jails.

This, incidentally, is a recurring theme in the Narnia Chronicles. *The Lion, The Witch and the Wardrobe* tells how Aslan, with the help of Edmund, Lucy, and their older brother and sister, free the land of Narnia from the enslavement of the evil White Witch. *Prince Caspian*, set centuries after the defeat of the White Witch, recounts how the prince, again with the help of the English children, must defeat the oppressive regime of his corrupt uncle Miraz. That Lewis would revisit this theme—of liberation—again and again, speaks to how much he recognized liberation as a central element of the Christian faith.

In chapter three of *The Voyage of the Dawn Treader*, Pug the slave trader is the symbol of evil, whereas in chapter four a new and different personification of sin appears: Gumpas, the governor of the Lone Isles. We learn from Lord Bern that Gumpas pays lip service to Narnia, but in fact is a law unto himself—and a flimsy, pathetic, corrupt law he is. Surrounded by ill-kempt guards who seem to have no discipline and even less self-respect, Gumpas has capitulated to criminals and thugs such as Pug, simply because there is economic advantage in doing so. He is a chicken-hearted man, but also pompous and fond of throwing around what little weight he has. While Pug is unapologetically evil, Gumpas represents a different, and arguably even more insidious, brand of badness: the hidden corruption that loves to pretend to be good, even while it enables and allows true evil to flourish under its watch.

Lord Bern rightly counsels Caspian that if he wants to deal with the outright evil of Pug and the slave traders, he must first contend with the corrupt government, which means confronting and deposing Gumpas.

In real life the Gumpases of the world are not as easily overcome as in this tale, but sometimes in fairy tales good overcomes evil without a fight, and this is one of those times. By pretending to have a larger army at his disposal than he really does, Caspian quickly wins over popular support (no doubt because the common folks are tired of living in a lawless land), and then promptly cows Gumpas into submission, duly relieving him of his command and installing Lord Bern as the rightful governor of the Lone Isles.

While this is told with fairy-tale simplicity, it nevertheless contains a significant message: that evil truly is cowardly at its heart. While those of evil disposition may be dangerous and threatening when they have actual or perceived power at their disposal, Pug and Gumpas are, deep down inside, craven men who quickly give in when they believe that they are the weaker party in a conflict. Because of the cowardice of evil, those who ally themselves with good—whether that means Aslan in Narnia, or God in our own world—are assured of ultimate victory over evil, even if in the short term evil seems to win.

Speaking of Aslan, the noble Lion is conspicuous in his absence in this chapter. When later events in the *Dawn*

Treader's voyage bring first Eustace and then Lucy face-to-face with their own sin, Aslan appears. Why, then, does he leave Caspian and Bern to fight the corruption of the Lone Isles on their own?

We might answer this question in several ways. First of all, there is a difference between an individual's inner experience of repentance and the communal or collective struggle to fight evil that manifests itself in social or systemic ways. Perhaps if Gumpas or Pug had been truly repentant, Aslan would have appeared to them. But if this had happened, it would not have been part of the story as Lewis tells it. The author was enough of a realist to recognize that the struggle against social evil doesn't always have happy endings: reconciliation, while a Christian ideal, does not always happen, since it requires willingness on the part of all the involved parties. While we may hope that the perpetrators of evil will come to love Aslan (or Christ), those on the side of good have a responsibility to defeat evil, regardless of whether or not "the bad guys" experience a change of heart.

Second, Aslan (like Christ in our own world) is not in the habit of fighting our battles for us. If anything, the opposite is true: we are expected to fight on behalf of Christ (or Aslan). I don't mean this in a militaristic sense, but in the spiritual sense of contending against sin, injustice, abuse, and oppression. If we passively wait for Christ to show up and lead our battle for us, then we are simply trammeled by our fundamental lack of faith. Even in the seeming absence of God, we are called to do God's will—and this includes confronting evil where we find it.

Thankfully, the transfer of power in the Lone Isles happens easily and without too much fuss. But this chapter ends with Lord Bern suggesting to King Caspian that he abandon the voyage of the *Dawn Treader* and concentrate his efforts on ensuring that the Lone Islands remain free of corruption, particularly since the closing of the slave trade could mean a war with the unfriendly Calormens. Bern is, in effect, unintentionally tempting Caspian to abandon his spiritual calling. This is an ongoing threat in the spiritual life: the temptation to abandon our heart's desire, even for seemingly good reasons. In our own world, so much work needs to be done: feeding the poor, sheltering the homeless, protecting or cleaning the environment, working for peace and justice, assisting those who are physically challenged or intellectually disabled. While no true follower of Christ may simply turn his or her back on the demands of charity, never bothering to perform a single work of mercy (even cloistered monasteries offer hospitality to strangers and often engage in social work such as running food pantries), we have to remember that no one can ever hope to do everything that needs to be done. If we are not careful, we can become so immersed in the praiseworthy pursuit of justice that we abandon our own spiritual growth in the process. A worker for justice who lacks spiritual grounding soon becomes burnt out, bitter, or worse. Caspian is right to graciously turn down Lord Bern's request, leaving the lord with the task of ensuring that evil remains vanquished in the Lone Isles.

Caspian's destiny lies elsewhere.

FIVE

Through the Tempest

S THE *DAWN TREADER* sails away from the Lone Isles, having set the slaves free and established Lord Bern as the rightful governor of the maritime province, little has actually changed aboard the vessel itself. Eustace remains as unpleasant and selfish as ever. But Lewis turns his attention to Lucy and Reepicheep, who find the first few days sailing east of the Lone Isles to be just about perfect. The sea is delightful, the company wonderful, and the valiant Mouse amuses Lucy with games of chess (which she often wins because Reepicheep keeps wanting his characters to behave as fearlessly—and recklessly—as he himself would act in a life-or-death battle!).

Then one evening the ship sails into a storm, and a fierce one at that. For several days (Eustace claims "thirteen days" in his diary, but he is probably not the most reliable of witnesses) the ship struggles against the elements, and when finally the weather breaks, the *Dawn Treader* has lost a mast, one sailor, and much of her provisions. Having sailed too far to return to the Lone Islands on what meager supplies are left, the ship presses on, but its progress is hindered by a lack of wind.

Here C. S. Lewis points out that we must be careful after our initial victories against sin. Often new Christians, emboldened and enthusiastic by their initial resolve to live a sanctified life, will invest energy into amending their past mistakes and consequently will triumph over one or more of their habitual sins, sometimes even in a dramatic fashion— like the person who, following a spiritual awakening, successfully lets go of a debilitating addiction. But just as the *Dawn Treader* sails away from its successful routing of the slave traders headlong into first a severe storm and then several days marked by lack of wind (and progress); so too the ordinary spiritual life, even with a spectacular or hopeful beginning, easily runs into problems that threaten long-term perseverance.

A central element of Christian spirituality is prayer: opening our minds and hearts to God, seeking intimacy with God in love. *Meditation* and *contemplation* are, for Christians, types of prayer in which thoughtful reflection or silent awareness become means for seeking such Divine intimacy. But no matter how we pray, we soon discover that it is easy to pray, but it is very difficult to keep praying.

Many Christians find it surprisingly difficult to sustain a commitment to prayer, day after day. Both the storms and the doldrums of life seem to get in the way.

The storm that pummels the *Dawn Treader* reminds us of the vicissitudes of human emotions, where daily prayer can easily unleash powerful—and disturbing—glimpses into the shadow regions of one's heart and soul (C. S. Lewis penetrates even further into this potential pitfall of the spiritual life in chapter eight). The becalmed days afterward point to another problem, one that has its own technical name in Christian spirituality: *acedia*, which encompasses boredom, listlessness, and torpor in prayer, that in turn leads to an extinguishing of initial fervor and negligence of one's spiritual commitments.

Just as the storm symbolizes the problem of spirituality that is hyperemotional or excessively excited—a spirituality based on feelings rather than on solid discipline—so do the becalming waters of acedia point to the problem that ensues when the spiritual life becomes so devoid of emotion that it becomes lifeless, arid, and seemingly pointless. Both of these situations are dangers, and both function as temptations to abandon discipline in one's spiritual practice. The storms of emotions make discipline seem unnecessary, while the dryness of acedia make it seem pointless.

As the ship slowly moves forward, Lewis turns his attention back to Eustace, who disregards the water rations and is caught by Reepicheep trying to steal water at night. Blustery and defensive, Eustace refuses to accept responsibility for his actions, and only Caspian's diplomatic willingness to overlook the infraction puts an end to the conflict. Up until now, Eustace has been predictable in his narcissistic way of relating to everybody and every situation on board. But as the *Dawn Treader* makes its way at long last to an island for rest and repairs, Eustace is about to undergo an adventure that is uniquely his.

To Eustace's way of thinking, coming ashore after the harrowing experience of the storm should mean having time for rest and relaxation (apparently it didn't occur to Eustace that while he rested, someone else might have to keep working). Annoyed to discover that Caspian and the crew expect everyone to work hard on the many repairs needed for the ship, Eustace decides that he would rather enjoy taking a little walk. Convinced that he would not even be missed, he simply slips into the forest beyond the island's beach and meanders through the woods, eventually climbing a ridge to the top, where he enjoys a commanding view of the island. But here he also discovers something new: the experience of solitude, real solitude, perhaps something he had never fully experienced before. And to his great surprise, his self-imposed solitude leaves him feeling lonely.

Eustace had been so focused on relating to his cousins and other companions by criticizing them and holding them in contempt that he was, in essence, oblivious to the fact that he was part of a community—a gathering of people united around a similar mission or purpose. As Eustace saw it, he never asked to be involved with this community, he never volunteered to join the crew of the *Dawn Treader*, and so therefore he wanted no part of it. And it took the experience of feeling lonely for him to reconsider his position.

Sin causes alienation. It is easy to think of sin in a purely legalistic manner—as disobeying God's law—but the point behind "God's law" is to knit God and all humanity together in bonds of charity and love. Whether sin is personal or social in nature, it disrupts the flow of love in our lives. Think of how racism separates people of different ethnic backgrounds, or how an affair can destroy a marriage. Even when I was a little boy, I learned that telling a fib left me filled with fear: the fear of being "found out." But part of the nature of sin is that it blinds us to the very alienation we suffer. It is only when Eustace discovers the gift of silence and solitude (even from the most selfish of motives, to avoid legitimate work) that he begins to recognize the reality of such alienation at work within himself.

To a person who engages in meaningful spiritual practices, including prayer, meditation, and contemplation, silence and solitude are joyful experiences, doorways into the hidden communion with God. But for someone who is unaccustomed or resistant to the call of the Holy Mystery—

even a committed Christian—solitude and silence can feel uncomfortable and perhaps can even lead to anxiety or panic. This happens to Eustace, as his deep-seated distrust of others causes him to think that the ship may have left the island as soon as the crew realized he was absent. Gripped by fear, Eustace tries to run back to the beach— but disoriented by his emotional turmoil, he soon becomes lost in the jungle.

Just as relationship with God is the source of love in our lives, so alienation from God sooner or later leads to fear, or panic, or existential dread. By reaching this point, Eustace is actually coming very close to the most significant event of his life.

SIX

How a Boy Became a Dragon

NE OF THE GREAT heroes of Christian spirituality is Saint Benedict, who is the patron saint of Europe and the founder of the Benedictine tradition of monasteries (intentional communities devoted to a life of prayer). The motto of Benedictine spirituality is *ora et labora*—a Latin phrase that means "prayer and work." To Saint Benedict and his followers, true spirituality involves more than just blissful experiences of communion with God. There is also a necessary, and healthy, emphasis on life's ordinary responsibilities—on making sure there's food on the table and that the dirty dishes get washed. Eustace, whom we left at the end of the last chapter lost in the woods of an unfamiliar island, has not yet discovered the spiritual value of plain old-fashioned work. But at the moment, this is the least of his problems.

The crew of the *Dawn Treader* puts in a good day's work and finally sits down to a delicious feast, complete with the roasted meat of wild goats killed by several of the ship's archers. Only then do they realize Eustace is gone. Despite Eustace's paranoia that the others are waiting for a chance to abandon him, in truth as soon as they realize he is missing, they organize search teams to find him. And the fact that more than a few of them grumble about having to do this says more about Eustace's narcissistic behavior than about his basic worth as a person.

Here, C. S. Lewis shows us how human alienation— including the twisted psychology of narcissism and contempt for others—represents a fundamental distortion of reality. Eustace is so blinded by his disdain for others that he can only assume that they feel the same way about him. He cannot comprehend that others might criticize his behavior, but still value him as a person.

These are not the thoughts Eustace entertains as this chapter unfolds, for in his disoriented state, he is more immediately (and understandably) concerned about his safety. But if anything he digs himself even more deeply into his self-centered ways of thinking. Lost in a fog-shrouded valley, the boy discovers to his horror that he has stumbled headlong into a dragon's lair. As it turns out, the dragon of the lair is dying, and Eustace watches as it passes away. The relief that he feels as this particular threat subsides simply feeds his distorted way of seeing things, and before long he has convinced himself that he has actually *defeated* the great lizard.

"Denial is not a river in Egypt," or so the clever saying goes—but denial *is* something that anyone can easily fall into. In denying his sense of loneliness or vulnerability, Eustace is, in effect, lying to himself. He is a youthful symbol of the many ways we lie to ourselves: from alcoholics who insist their drinking is no problem to the compulsive shopper who believes it's no big deal to run up a huge credit card bill.

Soon the skies open and rain begins to fall, and so Eustace takes shelter in the dragon's cave, where he is surprised to find a hoard of treasure (Lewis loves to poke fun at Eustace's naïve lack of knowledge of mythical and magical stories, noting that he is the kind of boy who has "read only the wrong books"). Because he is Eustace, he immediately claims all this treasure for himself, and slips a large gold bracelet onto his arm. Tired, he falls asleep—and then his adventure takes a truly unexpected turn.

He wakes to find his arm throbbing with pain, and notices on either side of him what looks to be a dragon's leg. He also recognizes the smoke of a dragon's breath, right there with him in the cave. Cursing himself for his foolishness, he supposes that the dead dragon had a mate, and that Eustace is lying next to one (or two!) of the terrible beasts. Frightened, he bolts for the pool of water next to where the body of the dead dragon lies, and only when he gazes into the water—and sees a dragon gazing back—does he realize the horrible truth: somehow, during the night, he himself has been magically transformed into a dragon.

"For where your treasure is, there your heart will be also," said Jesus (Matthew 6:21). Eustace's heart, lost in greed by the lure of the dragon's hoard, had turned dragonish, and the rest of him followed in the transformation. Finally, the pompous, self-obsessed, arrogantly narcissistic little boy has discovered the fruit of his own deeds and values and choices.

Of course, in the real world no one turns into a literal dragon, but there are many ways in which we can become dragonlike, especially when we allow greed or fear or some other self-centered perspective to define us. Think of poor Mr. Scrooge from Charles Dickens's *A Christmas Carol*: after a lifetime of thinking and acting like a miser, he had become almost as much of a dragon as Eustace. A series of ghosts had to literally scare the hell out of him in order for Scrooge to turn his life around. As we will see, Eustace has a gentler path to renewal, although not without his share of suffering.

Ironically, though, beginning at this terrible moment of clearly seeing himself for what he really is, Eustace finally takes responsibility for his actions, and begins to change. Despite his fearsome appearance, and a momentary thought of using his dragon powers to "get back" at Edmund and the others, Eustace weeps for realizing how lonely he feels—and how this was all, really, his own doing. In those tears he finds the first glimmer of what Christianity calls repentance, from a Greek word that means "changing directions" or "changing your mind" or even "adopting a higher awareness." Having wept his tears of sorrow, the dragon sets off to rejoin his companions from the *Dawn Treader*.

Chapter six ends with several tense moments, as the humans understandably see a grave threat in this dragon that suddenly appears. First Lucy, then Edmund and Reepicheep sense that it is not hostile and discover that it can nod or shake its head, and thereby communicate.

When we make careless, fearful, or greedy choices, they can isolate us and turn us into "dragons." But the cleansing tears of repentance pave the way for a new direction in our lives.

SEVEN

The Cleansing Waters

POOR EUSTACE. Even though up until now he has been a singularly unpleasant character, the combination of his newfound sense of remorse and his unfortunate metamorphosis has made him finally worthy of our sympathy. I don't like to admit it, but I know that there is a little bit of Eustace in me. My "inner Eustace" especially loves to come out and play when I'm tired, or angry, or worried about something.

I know a Trappist monk who once told me, "The monastic life is very simple. We fall down, and we get back up, we fall down and get back up." This is true not only for monks, but for all Christians. Life in Christ is not a shortcut to perfection; rather, it is a lifelong journey, complete with plenty of setbacks. Eustace's story—particularly what happens in chapter seven—is a reminder that, no matter how big a mess we get ourselves into, by the grace of God we can always make a change for the better.

It turns out that the gold bracelet Eustace took from the dragon's hoard belonged to one of the missing Narnian lords, Lord Octesian. So even though at the beginning of this chapter things look bleak indeed for poor Eustace—having been turned into a dragon by his own greedy inclinations— the fact that he has unwittingly discovered treasure related to the *Dawn Treader*'s quest offers a subtle lesson: that even our foibles and mistakes can be used by God to help us get to where we need to go, or even to fulfill our calling. This is something that many Christians discover over the course of our spiritual journeys: that the very wounds we suffer, even as a consequence of our own actions, often turn out to be blessings by which we can help and serve others. We can see this in two members of the ship's crew who become particularly kind to Eustace during his sojourn as a dragon: Reepicheep, who spends time simply being a companion to the dragon, and Edmund, who first greets Eustace after he is transformed back into a boy, and who helps him to make sense out of his encounter with the noble Lion Aslan.

Reepicheep and Edmund, as readers of previous Narnia adventures will know, both suffered their own wounding— Edmund in the battle against the white witch, and Reepicheep in the battle against the Telmarines (when he lost his tail). Both characters experienced healing (which is a good thing for Reepicheep, since a Mouse without a tail is a sad creature indeed), but it was by their wounds that they became particularly well suited to comfort Eustace during his ordeal.

Once people recognize that the dragon is Eustace, they all try to be as kind as possible to him, Lucy even going so far as to kiss him. But what is truly remarkable is how the dragon himself seems to embody a markedly different character than Eustace's old self. As a dragon, Eustace tries to be helpful to the work crews (even finding a tree to replace the damaged mast on the ship) and discovers that the only thing keeping him from lapsing into despair as a dragon is the pleasure he finds in actually liking (and being liked by) others. He learns an important lesson here: that it feels good to do good. Still, he is aware not only that the ship cannot very well carry a dragon, but also that he has been little more than a burden from the beginning of his voyage. So weighty is his concern about what the future might hold for him.

Although he couldn't have put it in so many words, Eustace is growing in two truly important aspects of the Christian spiritual life: repentance and humility. Humility, for Eustace, is nothing more than the ability to truly know himself (even in the pain of acknowledging his faults). But by doing this, he is empowered to make a true and meaningful repentance—turning away from his old patterns of being selfish and arrogant, and in so doing, embracing an entirely new way of thinking and being: a way anchored in love and compassion. This orientation toward love, incidentally, is what I believe St. Paul meant when he talked about the "mind of Christ" (1 Corinthians 2:16).

❦

Several days go by, and then, one quiet morning, Edmund is surprised to find Eustace, now reverted to his human shape. Eustace tells Edmund what happened to him, and through this conversation we, the readers, are invited into his dramatic encounter with Aslan—an encounter that not only heals Eustace of his dragonish form, but also truly changes him forever.

Aslan, as I have already noted, is the true hero of all the Narnia Chronicles. He is a Lion, but not just any lion. Merely hearing his name evokes a sense of wonder in the hearts of his friends, but disconcerts those who oppose him. Encountering Aslan is always a life-changing experience, as Eustace discovers in a most dramatic way.

The last night he was a dragon, a Lion came to Eustace. Even though it was a moonless night, the Lion seemed to glow, with a light that appeared to come from the Lion himself. And even though Eustace was a dragon, he felt afraid—not afraid of being eaten, just—*afraid*. But the Lion did not hurt the dragon; on the contrary, he told Eustace to follow, and he led him to the top of a mountain where, in the middle of a garden, there was a well or a pool. The Lion instructed Eustace to "undress," meaning to claw away his dragon skin. Eustace tried, but after peeling several layers of the dragon hide off, realized he could only dig so deep into the scaly skin that covered him. So then the Lion took over, and began to claw away the skin. Frightened but desperate to remove his dragonish form, Eustace submitted—and found that the Lion's claws hurt like nothing he could imagine. But it was a cleansing pain, for with each tear of the claws, more of the awful scales and hide were ripped away. Finally the Lion threw Eustace into the pool, and the cleansing waters felt wonderful. Then, tenderly, the Lion dressed the boy in new clothes—and suddenly he was with Edmund, telling his story, wondering if it were a dream.

Edmund, who knew perhaps better than anyone on the *Dawn Treader* about facing up to Aslan after doing bad things, helped Eustace to see that this was no mere dream, but rather a mystical encounter with the majestic Lion himself.

The conversation between Edmund and Eustace is symbolic of the kind of one-on-one relationship known as spiritual direction or spiritual accompaniment, in which a person young in the spiritual life turns to an older companion for insight, advice, and encouragement. The companion helps the seeker to be more attentive to the movement of the Holy Spirit in his or her life—for, in Christian terms, only the Holy Spirit is the true director of souls. Edmund invites Eustace to recognize that he has experienced more than "just a dream," and helps him to make sense of the spiritual lesson to be found in his experience.

Although Edmund doesn't say so (and neither does C. S. Lewis), it's easy to see the cleansing of Eustace in the pool as symbolic of baptism—the sacrament of initiation into the Christian life. Spiritually speaking, baptism is the means by which we are adopted into the family of Christians— what tradition calls the Mystical Body of Christ. So, too, Eustace's immersion into the healing and cleansing waters is the culmination of his transformation from spoiled brat to a more mature, caring, and even loving person.

Lewis wisely points out that Eustace, while having undergone a genuine change of heart, is by no means perfect, and occasionally lapses into his old, ornery self. So it is with all of us: conversion in Christ is a process, not a simple one-time event. Christian spirituality is anchored in the idea that our entire lives are given over to a long, slow process of joyful conversion and repentance. Eustace embodies this, but although he does not become perfect, he clearly has turned a corner, and for the rest of the voyage is for the most part truly a new creation, thanks to the grace he received from Aslan—in the cleansing waters.

Danger after Danger

HE JOURNEY continues. At first everyone is of good cheer, glad enough to leave the dragon's island behind them. Now, no sea adventure would be complete without a visit to a deserted island, and this is the point in the *Dawn Treader's* voyage when that happens. But this particular uninhabited island yields nothing other than a small coracle, just the right size for Reepicheep, who decides to keep it. For those of you who have not read *The Voyage of the Dawn Treader*, I don't think I will be giving away too much by saying that this little boat will be very important for Reepicheep before the story ends. For our purposes, looking at the spiritual lessons hidden in this tale, the message here is obvious enough: even random elements discovered at one point along our journey might prove to be very beneficial later on. For example, there's the story of Sara Miles, who as a young woman was an atheist who just happened to loved to cook. Little did she know that one day she would encounter Christ—and discover that her passion for feeding people led her to set up a food bank in her church. When Jesus said "Feed my sheep," Sara took his words to heart, and began a ministry that touched the lives of hundreds of people. Like Reepicheep or Sara Miles, we need to keep our eyes open, for even the smallest event, relationship, or passion in our lives could be used by God to create something new and wonderful—all in the service of love.

The *Dawn Treader* sails on, and soon the crew find themselves burdened by boredom, when a day filled with rain leaves them cramped inside the ship's quarters. Eustace's old disagreeable self returns, and even Edmund begins to make cranky comments. Spiritually speaking, this is just another reminder that we will keep making the same mistakes, over and over again. Some wisdom can be found in learning to be especially mindful of our own actions (and extra forgiving of others) during such challenging times.

But the shipmates soon have little time to worry about boredom, for as the rain storms lift, the ship encounters what first looks like a series of odd rocks in the water—but what is soon to be revealed as the undulating body of a terrible sea serpent.

The monster tries to encircle and crush the ship with its body, and only the combined efforts of every member of the crew allow the *Dawn Treader* to escape—by literally pushing the coil of the serpent away from the stern of the boat.

After that close encounter, the ship sails on to a never-before-seen island, where a landing party makes an unpleasant (and nearly fatal) discovery. Near a pool of water, they find the armor of a Narnian lord—presumably, one of the seven missing lords. In the bottom of the pool lies what appears to be a life-sized golden statue. Thankfully, and by sheer chance, they discover (before someone dives in the pool or tries to take a drink) that the water must be enchanted, for anything it touches turns to gold. With a shudder, they realize that the statue at the bottom of the pool is actually a body—the missing lord, his corpse forever turned to gold.

Caspian, dazzled by this Midas-like discovery (and, presumably, unfamiliar with the myths of Greece, and so unaware of the horrible price that King Midas paid for his ability to turn things into gold), immediately claims the island—and the pool—for himself. Not only that, he threatens his companions, on pain of death, not to tell anyone of their discovery, not even the rest of the ship's crew. Stunned by the king's sudden display of avarice, Edmund challenges his presumption, and just when it appears that a fight will ensue, Lucy—and then everyone else at the pool—sees a vision of Aslan. Everyone is transfixed by what they see, and when the vision passes Caspian admits that he has been acting poorly. Reepicheep suggests that the island and the pool are cursed, and so the party returns to the ship—but their minds seem confused, and so they sail on, knowing only that one of the missing lords has died on the island, and that it is an accursed place, forever after known as Deathwater.

These adventures represent how the ongoing spiritual journey continues to involve real dangers. Of course, you and I are not likely to encounter threatening sea monsters or deadly waters, but serious obstacles nonetheless await anyone wishing to progress in the spiritual life. Both the sea serpent and Deathwater Island represent problems that rise up from within, problems that can thwart our ability to grow in grace. Like sea serpents, hidden dimensions of our subconscious or shadow can overwhelm us as we seek to progress in the calling of the spirit: love can be swallowed up by fear, peace by anxiety, joy by cynicism and bitterness. Our best intentions can be crushed by unhealed wounds or unmet needs from our own past, or perhaps even from the reptilian depth of the collective human psyche. For example, I am by nature an introvert. I do love people, but like most introverts, I need plenty of alone time to replenish my energy. Because of my personality type, I must continually monitor my hunger for solitude and make sure those needs are met, or else I am likely to become irritable and unpleasant when relating to others—and this helps nobody! My deep need for privacy will assert itself like a coiling sea serpent if I don't take preemptive steps to make sure my needs are met in healthy ways.

Likewise, the magical waters that turn things into gold symbolize the ever-present reality of temptations, attachments, and the lure of physical and spiritual materialism. We live in a materialistic culture, and the siren's song of ever new and greater possessions can swallow up our yearning for God and leave us simply hungering for more things—a hunger that "things" alone can never satisfy. It's not that God doesn't want us to enjoy the blessings of life—of course he does! But relationships, love, and loved ones are always more important than our material blessings, and our relationship with God is the most important connection of all. If we become so caught up in the race for possessions that we lose sight of the blessings of love, then we run the risk of suffering a spiritual death. Through personal initiative, the crew escape the sea serpent, but it takes a visitation from Aslan to break Caspian free from the entanglement of the Deathwater. Here we are reminded that grace is always necessary for us to avoid the dangers that await us as we travel along the way of Christ. Even though the crew apparently escaped the sea serpent without direct intervention from Aslan, it's worth remembering that the beast was not killed, only pushed aside—and left hungry. And this is often the case with the dynamics that threaten to derail the spiritual life, whether it is our sin or merely our innate selfishness: even with grace, such things are never vanquished, but remain a part of us always.

We are now at the halfway point of our adventure. From here on, the splendor and the mysticism—and the mystery—of this wondrous sea voyage will become deeper and deeper.

NINE

Voices in the Silence

THE SPIRITUAL LIFE is about transformation. When we sign up to walk with Christ, we receive a tremendous opportunity: to learn to love like Christ loves; to learn to think like Christ, to make Christlike choices, and to slowly, gradually, surrender anything within us that holds us back from such a life of love. But these changes come slowly. The transformations we undergo in our slow passage to holiness will be so subtle and so incremental that many people (including ourselves) might miss them altogether.

As the *Dawn Treader* leaves Deathwater Island, some of the crew think the morning sun looks larger than it did at the beginning of the voyage—but others disagree.

But in fact, those who think the sun looks bigger are right. It's not that the sun has gotten larger, but that the voyagers have come closer to it. But of course, the adventure is only halfway over, so there's plenty of perseverance—"stick-to-it-iveness"—that will be required in the days (indeed, months) to come.

The ships sails east into the morning sun so long that the crew begins to worry once again about its dwindling supplies. On the very last day before prudence would require them to abandon the quest, an island appears before them. The voyagers sail into a welcoming harbor and land—but what a strange land it is that they discover.

To begin with, it is silent and still, and apparently empty. But this is not a wilderness sort of silence, or the emptiness of an abandoned or untamed island: the landing party finds immaculately mown lawns and carefully tended trees, even though it is so quiet that all anyone can hear is the occasional cooing of birds. In the distance in this parklike place they see what appears to be a house; as they approach it, everything is so still that Eustace wonders if it is empty, but then Caspian points out a column of smoke ascending from the chimney.

This island, so C. S. Lewis tells us, is the island of the voices, but for a moment let's linger with the initial descriptors the author gives us: silent, still, peaceful, no noise. He repeatedly points out that, while this island appears to be well-tended and cared for, it is characterized by *silence.*

If *The Voyage of the Dawn Treader*, taken as a whole, represents the Christian spiritual life, then coming to this particular island—especially after all the adventures dealing with both social and personal sin, and the kinds of temptations and dangers that threaten those who undertake this journey—represents the heart of a disciplined prayer life. For sustained and disciplined prayer eventually reaches a place of profound silence.

Prayer begins with words: offering our thoughts and feelings to God. But there's more to prayer than just saying prayers. Great mystics down the ages have reported again and again that the spiritual life eventually leads to meditation (thoughtful reflection on God and God's purpose in our lives) and contemplation (where even thoughts are gently laid down, so that God's mysterious presence may be encountered in silence). The *Dawn Treader's* reaching the island of the voices, with its atmosphere of deep quiet, symbolizes that point in the spiritual life when our wordy prayers and meditations begin to shade off into the splendor of deep and restful silence. As its name implies, the island of the voices is not *entirely* silent. Everyone hears the pigeons coo. And Lucy, momentarily separated from the others, discovers something that, especially at first, seems truly ominous. She hears a mysterious thumping sound, unlike anything she's ever known. She cannot see anything making this strange noise. But then she realizes that disembodied voices accompany the thumping—and the more she hears what the voices have to say, the more alarmed she becomes. The voices—for there are several of them—speak of plotting to cut the *Dawn Treader* party off from any hope of returning to the ship. Whatever these unseen creatures are, they sound hostile—and ready to fight.

Lucy runs to catch up with the rest of the party and breathlessly explains all she has heard.

No one relishes the prospect of fighting invisible foes, so the only sensible thing to do seems to confront the voices and find out what they want. As it turns out, the mysterious voices seem far more interested in talking than in fighting. The chief voice recounts a long story of his people having been "uglified" by a magician who governed the island, and then made invisible by a spell that backfired. To lift the spell, they need a girl—Lucy—to go upstairs in the house, find the magician's book, and reverse the spell. Lucy, with Reepicheep's support, agrees to the task, and the chapter ends with the voices, no longer threatening, eagerly offering hospitality to the bemused Narnians.

It seems that as soon as we embrace the depth of silence that is necessary for disciplined prayer, we encounter "voices." The voices may not be as hostile as those on this magical island first seem to be, but they do threaten us in a specific way: they threaten to distract us from our purpose. These voices, you see, are nothing more than our thoughts—all of which come from deep within us. Clamoring for attention, they bring a myriad of needs and wants and desires. They convey anxiety, or anger, or desire, or perhaps other emotions. They subtly and not so subtly beckon and beguile us away from prayerful silence, often by giving us a list of things that need doing.

Should we just give in to the demands of persistent voices, the way Lucy agrees to their request? I won't answer that question right now, but I will note that fighting them is no answer. If we fight the distractions that keep us from our silent prayer, they will, unfortunately, just keep coming. We have to find another way of dealing with the voices in the silence. And indeed, the adventures on this Narnian island will give us a clue how to do just that.

TEN

Lucy's Temptations

HOSPITALITY IS a beautiful thing. Some of my fondest childhood memories center on the excitement in our home around holidays such as Thanksgiving, when out-of-town relatives would come to visit and we would all enjoy a huge feast. Then the following year, it was our family's turn to travel—and enjoy the hospitality of my aunt and uncle. Saint Benedict praised hospitality, instructing his monks that "guests who arrive should be received as if they were Christ."[6] Although it's not the last time this theme will appear in *The Voyage of the Dawn Treader*, chapter ten begins with a moment of hospitality—and it is a most amusing scene.

6   *The Rule of Saint Benedict*, translated by Carolinne White (London: Penguin Classics, 2008), chapter 53.

No longer sounding combative, the invisible people, thrilled that Lucy has agreed to their request, now offer a sumptuous feast to the *Dawn Treader* crew. But the shipmates soon find themselves tiring of the endless— and endlessly inane—chatter of their unseen hosts. The voices offer only the most bland and uncontroversial of opinions, and eagerly agree with each other, no matter how obvious the point being discussed. Finally, satiated on the fine food and mead, the crew retires for the evening.

The next morning feels like the day of an important test to Lucy. After breakfast and a final set of instructions from the chief of the invisibles, she climbs the stairs alone. Once again, the overall quality of silence, a silence that plumbs far deeper than the silly chatter of all the distracting voices, fills Lucy's awareness. As she ascends the stairs, the stairwell seems so still that all she can hear is the ticking of the downstairs clock. But on the second floor of the house, everything is so quiet that she becomes aware of the pounding of her heart. Even her feet make no sound, thanks to a thick carpet. Nervously she walks down the hall to the room where the magical book will be found. She enters the room, a library, and finds the book—large and handlettered. With no instructions as to where in the book she will find the spell needed to make invisible things visible, she begins to flip through it.

All sorts of spells can be found in this magical tome—from the most mundane (how to cure warts) to the most tempting (how to make oneself beautiful beyond description). Lucy, like most of us, is not immune to the beguiling promises that these spells dangle in front of her. When she comes across a spell that promised to reveal what your friends think of you, she impulsively decides to recite it, for purely selfish motives. No sooner have the words she spoke faded into the silence than a magical image in the book seems to come alive, giving her a glimpse of her best friend dismissing her behind her back. Angry and tearful, Lucy turns the page, where she discovers a story that promises to refresh the spirit. She reads it, and feels deeply soothed by it, although she could never remember it thereafter, except that it concerned a cup, a sword, a tree, and a hill.

Finally she sees the spell to make things visible, and recites it, and in doing so, finds to her delight that Aslan himself appears—called into visibility by her own words.

In many ways, Lucy represents the heart of the entire Narnia series. Although she appears in only five of the seven books, she is the most important character of the Chronicles besides Aslan. Among her brothers and sister, she is the one who sees Aslan the most and who apparently has the most intimate relationship with the great Lion. Much of the plot of *Prince Caspian* revolves around how Lucy would receive sightings of Aslan while others did not. For Lucy, this included a bitter lesson, for whenever Aslan's guidance directed her to follow one path, but her human companions insisted on going another way, trouble inevitably would ensue.

So Lucy, despite her youth, represents a person with a deep and mature love for God. But like all people, hers is not a flawless love, and the charms and snares of the magician's book prove to be too much even for her. This chapter, then, functions as a sober cautionary tale. It reminds us that no matter how long-standing and mature our life of prayer might be, we remain susceptible to temptations and pitfalls.

Climbing the stairs in the magician's house may represent the classical notion of progress in spirituality as a form of ascent. Several great writings of Christian mysticism have imagery of climbing or ascent in their titles: *The Ladder of Divine Ascent* by John Climacus; *The Ascent of Mount Carmel* by John of the Cross; *The Stairway of Perfection* by Walter Hilton. As we move deeper into a life given over to silent prayer, meditation, and contemplation, we are, in a sense, moving up in God's world. When Lucy reaches the landing, she notices that the house, if anything, has become even more silent. She has moved more deeply into the silence—symbolic of the silence of a sustained practice of contemplative prayer. But this is not a silence where only rest and delight is to be found. Rather, in the pages of the magician's book, Lucy faces the most challenging temptations she will ever encounter in Narnia.

Her first temptation obviously plays to her pride: a spell to make herself beautiful. Of course, this is a temptation that just about anyone can understand. We live in a world where even celebrities fear they are not attractive enough, so no wonder Lucy (or you or I) might feel the desire to take a magical shortcut to a more alluring appearance. She barely resists it, thanks to an image of Aslan that suddenly startles her—out of her competitive determination to become more beautiful than her sister. Lucy's next temptation, to learn what others think of her, is really just a variation on this theme, for after all, aren't the desire for greater beauty and the determination to learn what others think of us both indicative of insecurity? The flaw of the magic is that it seeks to address such insecurity by appealing to pride, rather than by finding true security in God's (or Aslan's) love.

Here, alas, she gives in, and the consequences are disastrous. Only the wondrous story to refresh her soul soothes her sorrow when the spell doesn't play out the way she hoped. In contrast to the spell's horrible outcome, the story proves to be a mysterious and unexpected delight.

With symbols that are reminiscent either of the crucifixion of Christ (the grail cup, the cross as a tree, the hill of Calvary, and the centurion's sword), or, perhaps, of the basic elements of nature (the cup symbolizing water; the hill, earth; the tree, air; and the sword, fire), the story acts like a balm, given to Lucy to ease her pain. Yet even this lovely magic has a twist: she cannot reread the story. Perhaps this is a symbol of how in the mystery of time no one can cross the same river twice—or receive the exact same gift from God more than once.

When Lucy finally completes her mission and casts the spell to make hidden things visible, Aslan appears as well. Sometimes, it seems, our actions bring us face-to-face with God, even if we are not seeking such an encounter (and perhaps such an encounter is all the more likely when we aren't actively seeking it). The Lion reproves her for giving in to her pride, and refuses to let her avoid facing the consequences of her own behavior. But he also promises that he will tell her the soothing story, again and again.

When we, like Lucy, move higher and deeper into the silent mystery where hidden things can be made visible, the temptations we face become both subtler and more formidable. But in this place of contemplative quiet, we also encounter unimagined beauty and wonder (and, we can trust, Christ himself).

In the depth of our inner silence we face many fabulous and terrible possibilities—temptations of magic, power, beauty, and illusion. Christ challenges us to let go of these diversions, and will come to us when we ask for him to appear. But in his arrival he will also call us to face our own errors and selfishness, even though at this point in the journey, the sins we struggle with may be subtle indeed.

ELEVEN

What to Do with Dufflepuds

HEN ASLAN APPEARS to Lucy in the library, he says he wants to introduce her to someone: the master of the house. It is easy to forget this important dimension of spirituality: that a relationship with God leads to new, and deeper, relationships with other people. Concerning prayer, Jesus told his disciples to "Go into your room and shut the door and pray to your Father who is in secret" (Matthew 6:6). It is too easy to draw a conclusion that prayer, therefore, is a private matter, just between you and God. But Christian prayer, like every aspect of Christian life, has an important *relational* dimension. We pray not only to get closer to God, but also to open our hearts and lives so that God will draw us closer to our neighbors, our friends and loved ones, and especially those in need.

So Aslan introduces Lucy to a barefooted elderly man in a crimson robe, who bows before the Lion and welcomes him to "the least of your houses." Addressing him as Coriakin, Aslan speaks briefly with the magician, making a cryptic reference to stars resting in the islands. Promising Lucy that she will see him again soon—for to him, all times are "soon"—the Lion vanishes.

Coriakin offers Lucy a sumptuous meal, although he only eats bread and wine while she dines. As they dine, he tells her tales about how silly the "Duffers," the talkative (but, up until now, invisible) inhabitants of the island, have been—foolish, stubborn, and all but impossible to govern. When the meal is finished, they look out the window to where the Duffers are napping, and Lucy discovers to her delight that they are monopods—dwarves, but with only one leg, upon which they hop to move about (thus explaining the mysterious thumping noise they make). The magician explains that the "uglification" consisted of a spell to give them one leg instead of two, cast upon them to discipline them for obstinate behavior. Lucy resolves to explain to the Duffers that she thinks they are not ugly at all, but wonderful just the way they are. Yet when she attempts to tell them that, she soon gives up because of their sheer inability to listen.

Meanwhile, Reepicheep tries a different approach to dealing with the one-legged dwarves. He teaches the monopods a new trick—he explains to them that their one, large foot could serve admirably as a sort of boat or a ski, allowing them to skate along the surface of the water with marvelous speed and dexterity. Although the chief Duffer has his doubts, soon enough the monopods are joyfully floating on the water, their "uglification" apparently forgotten with their newfound appreciation of this unrecognized ability.

Coriakin helps the crew of the *Dawn Treader* perform necessary repairs on the ship, and tells them that the four still-missing lords did in fact visit his island several years earlier. Inspired, with their stores fully restocked, the ship sails on, the happy Duffers (now calling themselves "Dufflepuds" as a sort of blending of their original name and "monopod") cheering them on from the waters of the harbor.

What do the Dufflepuds teach us? At least one important lesson: we interpret our own experience—for good or for ill (and, in fact, how we choose to perceive what happens to us really does make a difference in the quality and meaning of our experience). In just over a day's time, Lucy and the *Dawn Treader* crew have gone from seeing the Duffers as threatening, to annoying, to finally rather silly and harmless. But consider how the Dufflepuds themselves were trammeled by their own limited perception: they were so afraid of Coriakin that instead of seeing him as a kindly governor, they became trapped by their own idea of him as a fearsome sorcerer. Rather than making the same mistake as the Dufflepuds, we can follow Jesus' advice, "Do not judge" (Matthew 7:1)—and choose to be slow to judge our experiences. By doing so, we can—unlike the Duffers—keep an open mind, therefore less likely to be trapped by the limitation of our always imperfect way of seeing things.

Since the island of the voices, with its character of deep and profound silence, can be seen as symbolizing a mature prayer practice, perhaps the silly little Dufflepuds are like the distracting thoughts that inevitably appear when we pray. They symbolize what Buddhists call "the monkey mind"—incessant mental static, chattery but largely inane thoughts and ideas and emotion-laden words that pop up over and over again whenever we seek to rest in profound silence as a way to pray to God without words. While great mystics throughout the history of Christianity have advocated silence (and silent prayer) as keys to the spiritual life, the sad reality is that time spent in silence is also usually time spent dealing with inner distractions.

Like the mental chatter that dances through our contemplative silence, the Dufflepuds are harmless but often annoying; largely meaningless, but quite insistent and demanding of our attention. Yet once we see them for what they really are, we recognize just how silly and funny they are. I know that when I seek to be present with God in silence, sometimes my monkey mind will assail me with matters I'm worried about, or with items on my to-do list, or even just random thoughts about a movie I've recently seen. Over time, I have learned that entertaining worries does little to assuage them, replaying a movie in my mind does not increase my enjoyment of it, and that the best way to deal with an urgent task is promptly to write it down (and then gently to return to my prayer). In other words, my silly little thoughts can easily derail my prayer time—or they can be laid aside, thus enabling me to return my focus to God.

Our distracting thoughts may seem like the insistent demands of a needy relative—and just might point to our own deep insecurities. We might find, like Coriakin with the Dufflepuds, that they simply do not listen to reason. Whenever such a thought succeeds in distracting us, our task is to simply and clearly return our focus to where it belongs: on the Divine Mystery we call God, and on God's deep and loving silence. Reepicheep's brilliant idea of teaching the monopods to use their big feet as little boats is reminiscent of an analogy that Thomas Keating, a popular Christian writer and teacher of contemplative prayer, uses to help people learn to manage their distractions. Keating suggests that we consider our thoughts to be like boats floating on a river. Our job is simply to watch the boats float by; not to worry overmuch about them, and certainly not to attempt to stop them. Indeed, the ultimate goal is to attend more to the clear, refreshing waters beneath the boats—in other words, to pay more attention to the silence between our distractions, recognizing that it is in the silence that we most fully find our rest in God.

The Dufflepuds love their newfound talent of skating on the surface of the water, and do nothing but cheer as the *Dawn Treader* sails on to its next destination on the voyage. Likewise, once we learn to be gentle but unattached with our distractions, they cease to annoy us and might even amuse us as we set our sights on relaxing deeper and deeper into the God we seek through prayer.

The Dark That Only One Light Can Pierce

THIRTEEN DAYS OUT to sea after leaving the island of the voices, the *Dawn Treader* crew see something that looks like a great "dark mountain" ahead and to their left. With no wind to propel the ship forward, the crew have to row through calm waters to reach what eventually is seen to be not a mountain, or even necessarily an island, but, simply, a "darkness." Out of the stillness of the waters without wind, the ship slowly rows into what first appears to be a mist, and then, increasingly, simply . . . darkness. As the ship sits at the edge of twilight, poised to enter into a darkness where no light can penetrate, the king and the crew balk at the idea of going forward. Only Reepicheep, the smallest being on board but clearly the largest in terms of his courage, speaks up to remind everyone that the purpose of the voyage is to seek adventure—and that to turn back now will reflect poorly on their honor. While a few of the crewmen grumble under their breath and Caspian openly expresses his annoyance with the valiant Mouse, they all recognize the truth of Reepicheep's words, and so, slowly, the ship begins to move forward into the dark, chilly, and silent blackness. Soon all sense of time and even motion seems to disappear into the impenetrable void.

Suddenly, a voice calls out. With shrieks and cries, it pierces the blackness, speaking in apparent riddles about dreams. Then arises the sound of someone swimming to the ship, and when a man, disheveled and panic-stricken, is pulled aboard, he urgently begs the ship to turn and run, for this is the island where dreams come true.

As each person on board realizes this means not only dreams, but nightmares too, the crew needs no further encouragement. Only Reepicheep the Mouse seems unfazed by the horror of having dreams come true. The crew rows as quickly as possible, but already in the silent darkness, each person starts to hear the bone-chilling sounds of their deepest, most primal fears. Various individuals on board begin to mutter that they are lost in the darkness, and will never make it back to the light. Despair seems poised to swallow up the ship, dragging each person aboard into the abyss of madness.

Lucy alone somehow manages to maintain the presence of mind necessary to pray to Aslan, asking for help. She realizes that even in saying her prayer, she begins to feel better. And help does come, in the form of a bird—an albatross, high above, that seems to emit a light of its own, and that looks almost like a cross when it first appears. Circling the ship three times, it seems to whisper to Lucy to have courage. That's when she understands that this is not just a bird *sent by* Aslan, but indeed is Aslan himself, in another guise, bringing hope and light and guidance toward the way they should go. Gratefully, the crew steer the vessel to follow the giant bird, and soon the dark gives way to twilight, and then to light, bright and glittering and free from the chill and the fear they have now left behind.

Finding themselves beyond the island where dreams come true, the crew learn that the man they rescued was yet another of the missing lords of Narnia. Finally picking up a refreshing breeze, King Caspian generously orders grog for all the crew, hoping that it will make every man that can be spared "groggy"—so that they might find restful, dreamless sleep. Meanwhile, no one, not even Lucy or Reepicheep, notices when the albatross has vanished.

Clearly, this spooky chapter offers Lewis's imaginative exploration of a key theme in mature Christian spirituality: the dark night of the soul. The great Carmelite saint John of the Cross wrote about how God leads those who love him through a dark night of the senses (when inordinate attachments to sensual pleasures are stripped away for the love of God) and then, the far more terrifying dark night of the soul—when even our most deep-rooted attachments to religious practices, to holy images, or to the basic structures of our own self-concept will all be dismantled in the interest of pure faith in God alone. The journey through the dark night is not for the fainthearted. Rather, it suggests a shattering, wrenching, initiatory experience in which all of our idols are stripped away, leaving us naked, vulnerable, and completely dependent on God, who alone can lead us into the demanding realm of deep interior transformation.

Lewis, of course, is telling a story, and one for children at that, and so he does not use any of the psychological or theological language traditionally associated with the dark night of the soul. Instead, he gives a much humbler, but truly powerful, metaphor for the dark night: a place where dreams come true. Everyone knows the chill in the gut that comes from a truly scary nightmare.

But the island of darkness isn't just about dreams and nightmares. It is about loss, about unknowing, about feeling like there is no way out. It is about the crisis of faith that comes when God seems truly, utterly, totally absent. Such feelings are normal, and even "great" Christians (such as Mother Teresa of Calcutta) have such experiences of the seeming absence of God. Likewise, the spiritual dark night experience is about getting in touch with our own shadow, the mysterious places within us where our fears, our inhibitions, our reptilian nature reside. Earlier in the voyage, we caught a glimpse of the shadow regions when the sea serpent came up and attacked the ship. But it was successfully fought off. Now, however, we face the scary truth that the serpent lives inside each one of us, and arises whenever we experience unexplainable fear, or rage, or jealousy. If the spiritual life is about total transformation in Christ, eventually even the darkest places within us must also be healed. Entering into those dark places can be a chilling experience. Such is the dark night of the senses— and the dark night of the soul.

Lucy discovers that the only way out is through prayer. Prayer in itself is a balm for her, but it also leads to hope coming from Aslan—except that Aslan appears in a way that he has never appeared before. This teaches us that the dark night strips away all of our attachments, including attachments to old beliefs about how God "should" appear and act. Because of Lucy's faith, and all of the crew's willingness to receive help (even from an unlikely source), the passage through the darkness comes to a happy resolution.

The Narnian lord represents a cautionary consideration that it *is* possible to get stuck in the dark night. This could be a psychological matter—depression, if unaddressed, can become an ongoing problem—or a spiritual matter (an existential crisis of faith can likewise linger for years or decades). When we enter our own dark islands, we need to be prepared to pray for the light of the albatross. This can (in fact, I would say *should*) entail reaching out for support from our friends, family, church community, and counselors. After all, we human beings bring Christ to one another. In the midst of the chilly darkness of unknowing and profound doubt, another person may be the only "Christ" we are capable of seeing, or holding on to. This is an important point to keep in mind.

The Feast, the Maiden, and the
Ultimate Quest

As THE SHIP SAILS ON, further and further away from the terrors of the darkness, the wind remains constant, although after some days it appears to become gentler and gentler, to the point where the ship merely seems to be gliding across water that seems more like a lake than a sea. Meanwhile, the night sky is filled with constellations that no one on board recognizes—and Lucy, with a shiver of awe, realizes that no living being may be familiar with these particular stars and the patterns they form. Then one evening as dusk settles in, the ship comes to a new island, one filled with rolling hills, beautiful colors reflected off of the setting sun, and a mysterious smell that Lucy and Caspian describe as "purple." They find a bay where the ship drops anchor and everyone on board (except the haunted lord rescued from the island of dreams-come-true) goes ashore. The meditative sound of the surf crashing on the shore can be heard throughout the island. Walking inland, the party soon discovers a marvelous site: a set of unroofed pillars surrounding a long table, filled with a sumptuous feast, but with no one eating the food—just three men, fast asleep, their beards and hair so long and unkempt that it appears as if they are all covered in hair.

The fearless Reepicheep investigates, and sees that the three are not dead, but only sleeping—and Lucy comments that they must be under some sort of enchantment, to have slept for so long. Their jewelry marks them as the last of the missing Narnian lords, but they cannot be roused from their slumber. Caspian, the English children, and Reepicheep all resolve to keep watch at the table during the night, and so they do, but no one touches the food, for fear it is under a spell. The hours of their long nocturnal vigil slowly pass by, silent except for the continual sound of the waves on the beach. Finally, just as the morning breaks, the *Dawn Treader* party sees a beautiful, elegantly dressed woman coming to them from a doorway in the side of a hill beyond the pillars. She carries a light, and as she reaches them Lucy notices a terrible-looking knife on the table.

The watchers all rise to their feet, instinctively recognizing the nobility of this lovely young woman. When she speaks, she asks why they have not eaten, and Caspian replies that they are wary of the food, thinking it caused the Narnian lords to sleep. The lady observes that the lords never touched the food, and tells the story of how they came to her island and quarreled about whether or not to return to Narnia, and one of them touched the knife—and *that* caused their perpetual sleep. With this, Lucy recognizes the knife—it was the very weapon that the evil witch had used to slay Aslan (as recounted in *The Lion, the Witch and the Wardrobe*).

Edmund speaks up and challenges the lady, saying he doesn't know what to believe: whether she is a trustworthy noblewoman, or merely a witch in disguise. He wants to *know* if she is their friend. But she mysteriously replies that they *cannot* know; they can only choose to believe—or not.

With this Reepicheep pledges himself to the lady, takes a drink of wine, and begins to feast. All the others join in, as the lady notes that this is called Aslan's Table since it was the Lion who decreed that it be set. The chapter ends with the lady and Caspian discussing what it would take to break the spell on the three sleeping lords, and the lady points to her father, coming out of the hillside doorway, which is now more visible thanks to the dawn.

As the first part of *The Voyage of the Dawn Treader* featured a symbolic baptism in the encounter between Eustace and Aslan in chapter seven, now we've come to the Eucharistic Feast: "Aslan's Table" is the Narnian equivalent of the Christian "Lord's Supper." And just as Christianity contains warnings against those who would eat the body and blood of Christ unworthily, so Aslan's Table has proved to be a stumbling block for the Narnian lords who sat at it and quarreled rather than gratefully partaking of the meal. Caspian and his crew, wary but respectful of this magical place, receive a beautiful vision of the maiden of the island, who invites them to believe—and eat.

Likewise, the Christian Eucharist—bread and wine consecrated as the body and blood of Christ—is a mystery that cannot be "known," only lovingly believed in (or not). Incidentally, the word "believe" comes from an ancient Germanic root word that means to "hold dear, love."[7] So I believe that the maiden was telling the voyagers they had a choice—between love and fear. Led by the faithful and fearless Reepicheep, the *Dawn Treader* party chooses to believe, and so partakes in the sumptuous food.

Notice that this chapter takes place largely over the course of the night. The "dark night of the soul" may have been left behind, but our heroes and heroine remain in the

---

7   Online Etymology Dictionary, http://www.etymonline.com/index.php?term=believe, accessed September 19, 2010.

dark night of faith—what one anonymous medieval mystic called "the cloud of unknowing." *The Cloud of Unknowing* is a medieval manual of contemplation that insists we can never fully know God (after all, God is bigger than the limits of human understanding), but we can be united to God through love. But it is a "dark" love, in that it requires us to reach out to God in faith. For times when God seems absent, or life is filled with pain, sometimes love is all we have to hang on to. But as surely as night gives way to the dawn, so we can trust, through our love, that every season of darkness will eventually yield to a glorious new sunrise, filled with beauty, and hospitality, and a wonderful feast.

In arriving at Aslan's Table and finding the last of the seven missing lords, one might say that the quest of the *Dawn Treader* has been completed. But as Caspian and his companions enjoy the feast, a shadow remains cast over the table, for the long-lost lords remain asleep and no one can rouse them. The beautiful maiden hints that the *Dawn Treader* crew will have one more quest to fulfill in order to wake the sleepers—as well as for Caspian to win an even more glorious prize.

And so it is with the Lord's Supper. The Eucharistic feast exists not just to nurture those who come to it in faith and loving trust. Rather, by its very nature, the sacred meal is meant to be given away; those who receive the call to be fed are then summoned to go forth and feed (love and care for) others. Never mind that the lords sleep by their own fault. All those who are nourished at Aslan's Table are given a quest in service of those who are in need.

We live in an imperfect world. Even for Christians who are dedicated to learning how to love like Christ, pain and suffering is never far away. Christ never promises to eliminate our suffering, but rather he can transform it, so that we can find meaning and purpose even in the dark places of our lives. But such meaning only really comes to light when we seek to give the love of God away—that is to say, love our neighbors as ourselves. Each one of us is called to love our neighbors in a unique way. Your call may seem very ordinary (as simple as being kind to the people in your life) or very dramatic (traveling to a foreign land to help those who are impoverished). At this stage of the spiritual journey, each of us must discern our own unique destiny, recognizing that the common denominator will always be love. For the crew of the *Dawn Treader*, this ultimate destiny means one more task: to help the three sleeping lords.

FOURTEEN

The Choice to Persevere

ADLY, C. S. LEWIS never tells us the name of the beautiful maiden, although Douglas Gresham, Lewis's stepson, christened her Lilliandil for the 2010 film version of *The Voyage of the Dawn Treader*. Chapter fourteen begins with the maiden and her father singing. They turn to the east, and as they sing, the sun rises. Amid the beauty of their song and the radiant rays glistening off the knife on Aslan's Table, Lucy and the others realize that the sun truly does appear *bigger*. There is no mistaking it now. After all, they are at the beginning of the end of the world. And from what seems to be out of the very center of the sun itself fly birds, countless white birds, that sing in response to the father and daughter's song, and they fly to the table and eat all the food. But one of the birds brings something blindingly luminous that looks like a burning coal or a piece of fruit, and gently lays it in the old man's mouth. Once the birds fly away, the old man introduces himself as Ramandu, an old star down from the sky and resting on this island. Each morning when the bird brings him a fireberry from the sun, he becomes a little bit younger, until the day when he will return to the sky and join the celestial dance. Ramandu notes that Coriakin, the governor of the Dufflepuds, is also a star, but one that, perhaps, has been punished for some unnamed infraction.

From the star at rest Caspian learns that, to awaken the sleepers, he must sail as far to the east as possible, and leave a member of his crew to continue the quest, before returning to the island. Acknowledging that the crew of the vessel might not embrace this final quest, Caspian informs the men that only some of them will be chosen to go. This bit of reverse psychology achieves its goal, and in the end only one crewmember is left behind on the island. But the lord rescued from the darkness is also left, alongside the three unconscious lords, to rest in dreamless sleep until the *Dawn Treader* returns. On their final night before departing to the "utter east," the entire crew feasts at Aslan's Table, and Caspian promises beautiful Lilliandil that he shall return, hoping to speak to her again. She looks at him and smiles.

The Eucharistic feast at Aslan's Table provides not only a lavish meal to the crew of the *Dawn Treader*, but also the rationale for their the final quest; and in this chapter we discover the terms of that challenge. Ramandu instructs Caspian to take his ship as far as possible to the end of the world, and to return—having left at least one behind to continue the journey without ever turning back.

What are the Christian implications of this chapter? The Eucharistic feast ultimately is related to the two great commandments: to love God, and to love our neighbors. Through loving God, we are called to persevere as far as we can on our journey toward holiness, toward complete surrender of our wills to God—toward what the ancient fathers of the church called *theosis*, or union with God. Some of us will not go as far as others on this most sacred of quests. But even if we ultimately cannot take this journey as far as we might hope, we are also called to support others in *their* destiny of attaining union with God. This is the true meaning of "love your neighbor as yourself." Help others to reach the ultimate goal that you yourself would love to reach, whether or not you do.

Of course, many of our neighbors might need love expressed in a more down-to-earth way: food to eat, clothes to wear, basic education or support in recovery from addiction, or simply just caring friendship and companionship. But these humble ways of loving our neighbors still serve the ultimate goal of persevering in love for God—for a hungry person is not in a very good position to attend to spiritual needs; we need to take care of our bodies as a prelude to caring for our souls (and we need to help each other in physical ways before we can support each other in spiritual growth). But "loving our neighbors" is not just about charity for those in need. It is also, ultimately, about helping each other to participate in the Divine Nature. A flower must have plenty of water and sunlight in order to bloom—and once it does bloom, its beauty blesses everyone who sees it. Humanity functions in the same way. When our physical needs are met, we are in a better position to "blossom"—to reach our fullest potential, whether that means developing a creative skill, supporting those in need, or in some other way living life to the fullest. Saint Irenaeus said in the second century "the glory of God is a human being fully alive." We fulfill our destiny to love each other whenever we help one another to become fully alive.

Caspian eagerly accepts the final quest, but recognizes that he cannot just force his tired and longsuffering crew to accompany him as far as possible to the end of the world. Likewise, no one can force anyone else to grow spiritually. Such a commitment must always come from within. But what would Caspian do if no one volunteered to assist him and accompany him on this final leg of the journey?

Here C. S. Lewis has his protagonists indulge in a little bit of psychological persuasion. Knowing that scarce goods are always more desirable, Caspian makes the journey to the world's end a privilege reserved only for those who truly deserve it—and then asks for volunteers. The same crewmen who have been grumbling the most audibly about how long the trip is suddenly are all but tripping over themselves trying to curry the king's favor!

But two persons do end up getting left behind: the haunted lord, and one lone crewman who has been the loudest grumbler of all. Not everyone gets to complete the journey. Spiritually speaking, this points to one of the first lessons of *The Voyage of the Dawn Treader*: God is always in control, and this means that things (even the nature of our spiritual experiences) don't always turn out the way we would like. This is not to say that God plays favorites, or that some people get more "spiritual goodies" than others. Indeed, such thoughts are simply not useful. Every person is given a unique set of life circumstances, challenges, and gifts. Just as not everyone is called to be a musician on the par of Mozart or an artist the caliber of Michelangelo, so not every Christian will be called to "go the distance" of becoming an extraordinary mystic like Teresa of Avila or Francis of Assisi. Not every person who embraces the life of prayer will reach the summit of total *theosis* (the experience of union with God), at least on this side of eternity. This is not bad news—even if it does seem to go against our society's emphasis on ambition, competition, and celebrity. Most Christians are called to simple, humble, ordinary lives of prayer and service.

Most Christians will take the journey only so far, and will eventually have to balance their quest for the ultimate experience of divine love with the urgent call to immerse themselves in the need and promise of down-to-earth human love. Of course, in the economy of grace, "love of neighbor" and "love of God" ultimately are two streams flowing from the same source.

This insight is in many ways a revisiting of the lesson of chapter one—the spiritual life is a calling. But whereas at the beginning of the story Lewis introduces us to a character (Eustace) who wants nothing less than adventure in Narnia, by this stage of the journey only those who truly want it are called to persevere on the spiritual path. Lewis plays this to comic effect in his tale of Caspian's art of persuasion, but in reality the message given here is good news—for even after the dark night we are always free to choose what we desire. If and only if we desire the totality of experiential union with God, then we *might* be called to enter the highest mysteries. Or, maybe not. At this point in the journey the dynamics of our relationship with God are fully a matter of God's call, and those who make it this far, no matter what shape their call may take, are happiest and most at peace when they choose to conform their will with God's.

FIFTEEN

Where the Waves Grow Sweet

As IT TURNS OUT, the island of Aslan's Table is the last stop that the *Dawn Treader* will make before the journey to—well, the very dawn itself. Once they sail beyond Ramandu's home, the crew cannot but notice that everything seems different. Every morning the sun seems larger and nearer, and each dawn brings with it the unearthly beauty of the birds flying to, and then returning from Aslan's Table. As they fly they sing the song of the stars, in a voice that sounds human but in a tongue no one can interpret.

If one word could be used to describe this final segment of the adventure, it would be "beautiful." The sea seems glorious, as does the sun, the birds, and the silence itself. If that sounds good to you, then relax and enjoy the story— for the beauty and wonder will only increase.

Marvels abound, here at the last Narnian sea. Everyone on board the ship seems to need less sleep, and silence characterizes each passing day. But it is not an oppressive silence, as if imposed by some angry authority figure who wishes to stifle expression. Rather, everyone on board freely embraces this silence, and each person instinctively speaks only in whispers with the others.

Meanwhile, the very water of the sea itself becomes clearer and clearer, until it seems as if the ship is gliding almost in a sea of liquid glass. Lucy easily sees the shadow of the *Dawn Treader* as it moves along the bottom of the sea, so well defined it is in contrast to the clarity and light that fills the sea and its bed. Entranced by the topography of the ocean floor, Lucy eventually realizes that an entire world lies beneath the water—and an inhabited world at that. Forests, roads, and even an underwater city and castle come into view, for the *Dawn Treader* is sailing above the home of the mer-people. Riding on seahorses and herding fish the way a human might herd sheep or cattle, the mermaids and mermen seem lordly and noble, and—as we will see in chapter sixteen—one young girl in particular makes a lasting impression on Lucy. Reepicheep, mistakenly thinking that one of the mer-people has behaved aggressively toward him, jumps into the water to settle the matter right then—only to discover, to his astonishment and delight, that the water tastes *sweet*. While this bit of news fascinates the entire crew, the sweetness causes particular exhilaration for the Mouse, for it recalls to him a prophetic word that a Dryad recited to him when he was still "in the cradle"—that where the waves grow sweet, Reepicheep will find all that he seeks—in the "utter East."

Indeed, it is that haunting rhyme from the dawn of his life that has inspired the chivalrous Mouse to participate in the voyage of the *Dawn Treader*, and that leaves him resolved to persevere in his journey to the east as long as he is able so to do.

As for the sweet water, quickly a bucket is lowered into the sea and Caspian drinks of the liquid. As soon as he drinks, the others notice a change about him—as if his entire countenance begins to glow. He describes the water as almost like *liquid light*. Then Lucy tastes the water and exclaims how wonderful it is, but that it seems so strong that no longer will she (or anyone else) need any food. And so then they all drink. And they fall silent.

And as everyone on board enjoys the water—the liquid light—their own eyes become more and better adapted to the dazzling radiance of the huge sun that blazes before them every morning. It is as if the very light itself has been caught, or embodied, in the waters of the last sea, and that somehow the water turns those who drank into light themselves, making the voyagers more capable of standing—and even gazing into—the luminous brilliance of the sun and of all their surroundings.

About this time, the crew notice that the air is perfectly calm, but that a strong current keeps propelling the ship forward. The Narnians begin to worry that this current might propel them directly over the edge at the end of the world. The English children respond by talking about how the world they come from (our planet earth) is not flat, but round like a ball. Caspian expresses delight that a round world exists, and the chapter ends on a humorous note.

⟨◦─⟩⟨⟨◦⟩

This poetic and delightful chapter celebrates several key images of traditional Christian mysticism, particularly those of silence and light. On one level, the second half of *The Voyage of the Dawn Treader* is a symphony of soundlessness, exploring how different types of silence can embody different spiritual qualities. From the silence of the Dufflepud island, filled with the distracting inanities of its residents, to the ominous stillness of the dark island, to the serenity of Ramandu's island, where the rhythm of the crashing surf provides a hypnotic soundscape, we have come at last to the mystical quiet of the last sea, where everyone voluntarily observes the deep yet luminous silence, creating a kind of reverence that we might associate with cathedrals or monasteries. This is the joyful peace of a mature contemplative life, a life that drinks deeply of the clear waters of the soul, where even one's own deep unconscious and shadow reside in a clarity provided by the brilliant yet safe light of truth. Compare the crystal clarity of the last sea with earlier descriptions of water: the storm out of which the sea serpent emerged; the treacherous pool that came to be known as Deathwater, and the foreboding dark waters surrounding the island where dreams come true. We learn through this voyage that much of what lies "in the depths" (whether of our subconscious, or of the mystery of the cosmos) remains hidden, and may well be dangerous. But now, having passed through so many trials and finding the humility to feast at Aslan's Table, and having become quite familiar with silence in its many forms, the *Dawn Treader* at last brings its crew to a place where what is above and what is below, what dwells in the air (the mind) and what dwells underwater (the heart), all serenely come together in a single radiance.

What, then, are these waters that at the last taste sweet, and that enable one to gaze directly into the light? This symbol could be tied to several dimensions of the Christian life: the waters of baptism, the waters of prayer, the waters of consciously choosing to live immersed in the Holy Spirit. It may not be necessary, or even particularly useful, to insist that this lovely plot element must correspond allegorically to some aspect or element of Christianity. C. S. Lewis resisted any attempts to make the Narnia books into allegories, and so let us follow his lead and choose not to make a hard and fast analogy here. We may simply see the "drinkable light" as symbolic of how a relationship with Christ is, ultimately, deeply refreshing and nourishing—recognizing that such nurture and inspiration can take many forms. William Blake once said that the purpose of life is to "learn to bear the beams of love." This is a great play on words, for a "beam" can be heavy (as a beam of wood) or weightless (as a beam of light). The summit of the Christian life brings us to a place where we "bear the beams of love" in all our relationships. Sometimes the beams of love seem heavy, as when we care for an elderly or chronically ill relative, or when we sacrifice time and energy to help out those who are in need. But the beams of love can be light, as well, as anyone in the delirious joy of newfound romance can attest. I believe that when we drink the light of Christ's love, we are called to carry both types of beams. And, like the waters' heart at the eastern seas of Narnia, these beams of love will refresh and sustain us, even as they give our lives meaning and purpose. May we all come to bask in such light—for Christ, after all, is the light of the world.

SIXTEEN

Meeting the Great Bridge Builder

 HE CAPTAIN OF the ship, Lord Drinian, warns Edmund and Lucy not to tell the others about the sea people, fearing that beautiful mermaids might seduce members of the crew, luring them to leap into the water where they would be lost forever. But before long the *Dawn Treader* sails into an uninhabited part of the ocean, although Lucy does see one more young mermaid, and in a fleeting moment of passing eye contact, feels as if she, and the sea girl, had become friends for all eternity.

"Eternity" is indeed the key word here, as the *Dawn Treader* sails on to the end of the world (with some of its passengers destined to go even further). We mortals might recognize that this last chapter of the book signifies a story coming to a close. But C. S. Lewis is showing us how the Christian life leads us to a place where time and eternity kiss.

For many days the ship continues to glide east, and the crew, nourished only on the winelike water, both feel rejuvenated and actually begin to appear younger. The emotional atmosphere on the ship seems a mixture of excitement and awe, in such a way that hardly anyone speaks, and rarely above a whisper. It is almost as if they are sailing not only to the end of the world, but also deeper and deeper into reverence itself—and into the very heart of a most sacred silence.

The voyagers notice a glimmer of something mysterious and white on the water ahead of them. As they sail on they realize that they are seeing a vast expanse of lilies, a special kind of blooming sea-lily that extends as far as the eye can see. Although Lewis describes these marvelous blossoms as white with the "faintest colour of gold," the voyagers decide to call this final stage of their journey the "Silver Sea." The flowers give off a lovely scent, and the water, visible where the vessel has pushed the plants aside, shines with a deep green color. And "shine" is the right word here, for everything seems to glow, especially given how huge the sun is now. But despite the dazzling brightness, everyone's eyes have adjusted so that all can see, perhaps more clearly than ever before.

The day finally comes when the sea becomes too shallow for the *Dawn Treader* to move forward. And while these last weeks have been marked by beauty and awe, one final moment of conflict threatens the travelers. King Caspian announces to his crew that they are to return to Narnia—without him. He has decided to join Reepicheep, taking the ship's rowboat and continuing the journey east to the dawn.

An unpleasant conversation ensues, as everyone reminds Caspian that his role as king prevents him from following whims that would take him away from his commitments and responsibilities. Caspian angrily replies that this means the quest is ended and the entire crew will return to Narnia. When Reepicheep reminds him that it *is* the Mouse's quest to continue to the east, the king storms angrily into his cabin.

And there he receives a visit from Aslan. C. S. Lewis does not show his readers this intimate encounter between the human king of Narnia and his leonine lord. We can only speculate how stern, and yet loving, Aslan is as he reproves Caspian for behaving selfishly at this climactic moment on the journey. Eventually Caspian emerges from his quarters, tearfully apologizes for his behavior, and—following the noble Lion's command—makes arrangements for Reepicheep, accompanied by Edmund, Lucy, and Eustace, to continue on their quest.

The sorrow of parting seems less important to Lucy than the joy she feels in the light, the silence, even the sense of solitude. Three days after leaving the Dawn Treader, Lucy, Edmund, Eustace, and Reepicheep come to a shallow spot where their rowboat can go no further. Directly ahead are wonders such as they have never seen before. At what they instinctively recognize is the very rim of the world stands a perpetual wave, like a wall of flowing water. And behind it, as the now vastly huge sun rises, they glimpse a range of mountains, filled with forests and waterfalls, that they all know in their heart is Aslan's country. And as they gaze at this heavenly sight, they hear music, the kind that "would break your heart" even though it isn't sad.

Reepicheep takes his little coracle, says goodbye to the English children, and paddles on alone. For a shining, brief moment, they watch him as he sails up and to the crest of the wave at the end of the world. And then he is gone—but Lewis assures his writers that he makes it into the majestic mountains and shimmering countryside of Aslan's country (a fact that is confirmed in the final Narnia story, *The Last Battle*). Mystery surrounds this dramatic moment: does Reepicheep die in the waves, only to be resurrected in Aslan's heavenly kingdom? Or dare we hope that the valiant Mouse has somehow crossed the line separating time from eternity, without the initiation of death? Lewis does not say, and I believe this is important—for this final chapter is not about heaven as someplace we go after we die, but rather about the many ways by which heaven comes to us and transforms our lives, even here on earth. After the sun rises, the vision of the mountains fades, and only the blue sky can be seen to the east.

But the children have something else on their mind, for they intuitively get out of their boat and wade to the south—and find land, and on this land is a Lamb, who invites them to breakfast. Then the Lamb changes into the form of Aslan, who speaks to them about finding a way into his country from their (our) world. Aslan says, "I will not tell you how short or long the way will be; only that it lies across a river." He also instructs the children that the purpose of their visits to Narnia is so that they might know him better—in our world. And then with a kiss and a blinding flash of light, they return to the bedroom in Eustace's house. One can almost see Lewis winking as he finishes the tale by assuring the reader that Caspian marries Ramandu's daughter, and that Eustace's change of character is permanent, much to his mother's chagrin.

The final chapter of the story, like the one preceding it, is filled with imagery of beauty and awe, of letting go but also of the peace that passes understanding. Lewis affirms that the Christian life is, finally, not a quest for Aslan's country, but indeed for Aslan himself. Confusing this subtle but important fact has been a perennial concern among the great mystics of the Christian tradition, and Lewis illustrates this final snare with Caspian's temper tantrum. Caspian, well-beloved son of Aslan, forgets the full nature of his calling and momentarily decides that he should accompany Reepicheep to beyond the very edge of the world, for no other reason than that he wants to. But the discernment of his companions immediately reveals that his motivations are narcissistic. Angry, he retreats and sulks; only a graced encounter with Aslan himself snaps him out of his fit. And so, at the end of the mystical journey, like the beginning, only God decides what form each person's experience of heaven (and of him) will take. Some are called to see the wonders of eternity, some are called to touch such wonders, and some are called directly into the experience of heaven. This is not our decision to make, and that can be painful to bear if we allow our selfishness (always present, even at this stage) to interfere with our quest for communion with God. We can become so dazzled by the gifts that are offered (especially gifts offered to others) that we take our eyes off the giver. And then, like Caspian, we may have to shed a few tears when we realize we can only be true to our own unique call, which may not always be to our egocentric liking. But just as Lilliandil, the lovely star-daughter, awaits

Caspian on his return, so too all who fully embrace their call will find unique blessings intended for them alone.

Meanwhile, Lewis uses Edmund and Lucy and Eustace to point out that even those who do seem to go the distance (for, although they do not *enter* Aslan's country, they *see* it, and break bread with Aslan himself) are often called away from the very gifts that have been given to them. Like these three youngsters, many contemplatives find that they are called out of the blissful experience of divine presence and back into the world where they may be of service.

Aslan promises the children that there is a way into his country from their world as well. He says it lies beyond a river, and critics have assumed that Lewis means the river of death, such as the mythological river Styx that one must cross to reach the underworld of Greek mythology. But I am not persuaded that this is what Lewis had in mind. Aslan could just as easily have been referring to the River Jordan—the waters of baptism. While many of us may not taste the fullest fruits of Aslan's country until after we shed this mortal coil, for an orthodox Christian like Lewis, the waters of baptism would have been the key factor in entering the life that leads to heaven. For whether we experience the fullness of heaven only after we die, or if by God's grace we are given a foretaste of it here, this, indeed, is the destiny, the glory, and the promise of the mystical life.

The Voyage of the Dawn Treader brings us, the readers, only within sight of Aslan's country. In the next volume of the Chronicles, *The Silver Chair*, the reader is invited into Aslan's land, but just briefly. Only one Narnian tale, *The Last Battle*, takes us fully into a celebration in Aslan's realm (and indeed, in that book, death plays a heart-stopping role).

The *Dawn Treader* brought its passengers (with the exception of the Mouse) only to the place where glimpses of splendor can be caught, in the midst of the silence and the light and the solitude. From there, all but Reepicheep were sent back to their homes, to their families and loved ones, changed (hopefully for the better) but living their transformed lives in ordinary ways. This, then, is the down-to-earth promise of the Christian life. We can assume that it is not God's intention to bodily assume us into heaven (like Enoch or Elijah or, for that matter, Reepicheep). If God does call us to a place where we can see the wonders of his homeland, it may well only be brief glimmers afforded in an overall life given to love (which, ultimately, is the heart of heaven anyway). And out of such momentary ecstasies, we are sent to serve others, to return from the end of the world (or the mountaintop) to put into practice our never-ending quest to love others as ourselves. For it is in love that God is most truly and assuredly known.

Conclusion

C. S. LEWIS ONCE wrote a letter to a ten-year-old girl—who had written him about a question she had concerning one of the Narnia stories—in which he explained, briefly, the meaning or the moral of each of the seven stories in the chronicles. When it came to *The Voyage of the Dawn Treader*, Lewis wrote that it was about "the spiritual life (specially in Reepicheep)."[8] This may be obvious to those who know the whole story, since the Mouse is the only one who "completes" the voyage. But all of the main characters in the story have plenty to teach us about Christian spirituality.

+ Eustace stands for the necessity of humility and repentance.
+ Edmund plays the wonderful role of a spiritual friend.

8 C. S. Lewis, *The Collected Letters*, Volume III (San Francisco: HarperSanFrancisco, 2007), 1245.

✦ Lucy, who is perhaps the most mystical of all the (human) heroes and heroines from throughout the Narnia stories, offers an important lesson of how even someone with a mature faith can give in to temptation—and then later in the story shows us how prayer and trust are the keys to moving through the darkest of "dark night" experiences.

✦ Caspian, the dashing and kindhearted leader of this adventure, nevertheless has to learn a hard lesson about how, in the end, the spiritual life is always and completely about obeying God's will.

✦ Reepicheep, meanwhile, functions almost like the hobbits in J. R. R. Tolkien's fantasies: the little person with a big mission, who embodies one of the most important of all Christian teachings: *Be not afraid.*

But perhaps just as important as all the various characters on the *Dawn Treader* are the various worlds that C. S. Lewis has created in order to lead us through the various stages of the Christian journey. Great mystics from ancient times have suggested that three stages define the spiritual life: purgation, illumination, and union. All of these are present in this story: the purifying lessons learned on the various stages of the journey (really, up to the very end, for Caspian is still being purified in the last chapter); the illumination that comes, first through the silence that gradually manifests itself over the voyage, then in the beauty of the star song on Ramandu's island, and finally in the lovely light and the healing water of the last sea; and most important of all, the union with Aslan, which is really just a culmination of a lesson that Lucy learns on the island of the voices: that Aslan is present in her life all along, and is ready to become visible to her, if only she will truly ask it of him. Likewise, here on earth, union with Christ does not require a spell to make hidden things visible—but rather, it is as a gift already given to us. To experience Christ's presence requires only that we seek his kingdom "within" or "among" us (Luke 17:21), that we endeavor to see him in our neighbors and in those who are in need (Matthew 25:34–40), and that we cultivate a regular practice of prayer, including meditation and contemplation (1 Thessalonians 5:17).

How do we make our own "voyage of the *Dawn Treader*"? Clearly, we will not visit Narnia except in our imagination. But we are all invited to make our own voyage to Aslan's— Christ's—country. Like Eustace, we need to begin by surrendering our need to be in control, our pride and arrogance, our impatience and lack of humility. Hopefully it won't take being turned into a dragon to learn these lessons! Like Edmund, we need to reach out to those in need, and be a friend when necessary. Like Caspian, we need to practice virtues such as generosity, hope, and, ultimately, obedience (a word that has become quite controversial in our day, but that in truth means *listening* for the whispers of God's instructions in our lives). Like Lucy, we need to keep the faith, trust that help and guidance will come when we need it, and be on guard against the subtle snares of spiritual pride. Finally, like Reepicheep, we need to be valiant, courageous, honorable, and always willing to stand up for what is right—and this could mean, for example, being honest even when it is uncomfortable to do so, or refusing to do anything that violates our conscience.

We need to follow in these characters' footsteps. And we need to persevere.

Like everyone aboard the *Dawn Treader*, we need to approach the spiritual life as if it were a grand adventure, a quest worthy of embarking on—a quest that will have its share of danger, but that will ultimately take us to a place filled with refreshing waters, nurturing silence, and dazzling light. We need to remember to whisper and allow ourselves to feel the awe of the presence of God (and we also need to remember that God is always present, even when we don't "feel" that presence).

Everyone's voyage to the land that lies across the river will be slightly different, for we are all unique. But like Eustace, we all need the cleansing waters of baptism; and like all the voyagers, we need the continual nourishment of the Eucharistic feast. Find a community where such nurture is available for you—and embark on your own quest.

Many blessings to you!

EVERYTHING I NEEDED TO KNOW ABOUT
CHRISTIAN SPIRITUALITY I LEARNED FROM
The Voyage of the Dawn Treader

1. Sometimes we choose to embrace the spiritual life, and sometimes the choice to walk the spiritual path is made for us.

2. Spirituality and mysticism do not, in themselves, make us into saints.

3. Everyone is at risk of being enslaved by sin.

4. The first order of business for anyone on this Christian journey: confront evil, set yourself (and others) free, and prepare for the adventures to come.

5. The journey will include storms—both external, and of our own making.

6. Our unloving choices isolate us—and turn us into dragons.

7. Even dragons can repent (all it takes is a little humility) and find new life through the cleansing waters of baptism.

8. The journey includes real dangers, from "sea serpents" (subconscious/shadow subversions, called up from the deep by the dynamics of the journey) to "magical waters" (temptations, attachments, and the lure of physical or spiritual materialism).

9. Eventually, the path of prayer will take us to a place of deep silence, stillness, and profound mystery, where invisible foes will threaten—or, at least, distract—us.

10. As we move higher and deeper in the way of silence, the temptations we face become both more subtle and more terrible—while we also encounter unimagined beauty and wonder (and, we can trust, Christ himself).

11. The way we interpret our experiences is at least as important as the experiences themselves.

12. The dark night is an unavoidable part of the journey. Filled with dreams and nightmares, it can only be traversed safely in the presence of Christ.

13. We are invited to the Eucharistic feast at Christ's table—and in doing so we will be called to serve those who are in need.

14. Not everyone follows the same mystical path. God ultimately decides what kind of spiritual experience we will have. For most of us, it's the journey, not the goal, that matters.

15. Wonders abound as we persevere on the journey; we see things from new perspectives and with greater clarity, enjoy greater light in our lives, and find sweetness in the most unexpected ways.

16. At the end, like the beginning, only God chooses who will experience his presence or come into his country, and how. And even those who do go the distance are often called out of the divine presence and back into the world where they may be of service.

Acknowledgments

Thanks to Ellen Hart, who first suggested that I read the Narnia Chronicles; to the students of my Protestant Mystics class at the First Christian Church (Disciples of Christ) of Atlanta, who joined in my enthusiasm for how *The Voyage of the Dawn Treader* functions as a template for the mystical life; to Linda Mitchell, who read the first draft and offered much encouragement; to Greg Brandenburgh, for his kindness; to Linda Roghaar, for doing things the old-fashioned way; to Mike Morrell, for plugging me in to his amazing network; to Jon Sweeney and everyone at Paraclete Press, for their support and hard work; to the monks and lay associates of the Monastery of the Holy Spirit, for being my spiritual mentors and friends; and finally and most importantly, to my family, Fran McColman and Rhiannon Wilburn, for their love, affection, and tolerance of my writerly quirkiness.

Appendixes

❦

Some Facts about
the Dawn Treader and Its Voyage

Cast of Characters

I
THE CREW AND PASSENGERS OF THE *DAWN TREADER*

King Caspian X ✦ The king of Narnia, who first appeared as Prince Caspian in the Narnian Chronicle of the same name. Caspian restored Narnia to justice after the reign of his corrupt uncle, Miraz the Usurper.

Lord Drinian ✦ The *Dawn Treader's* captain.

Edmund Pevensie ✦ English boy who first came to Narnia with his brother and sisters during the reign of the White Witch. Edmund fell under the spell of the witch and betrayed his family, but was redeemed by Aslan. After the witch's defeat, Edmund and his siblings reigned in Narnia as kings and queens before returning home.

Lucy Pevensie ✦ Edmund's sister and the first of the Pevensie children to visit Narnia; reigned as a queen of Narnia along with her siblings. Deeply devoted to Aslan.

Pittencream ✦ Sailor who is left behind on Ramandu's Island when the *Dawn Treader* sails to the very end of the world.

Reepicheep ✦ Chief Mouse of Narnia, who rose to fame during the battle to depose Miraz. Known for his honor, valour, chivalry, and seeming inability to feel fear, this talking Mouse rivals Lucy in his devotion to Aslan. He travels on the *Dawn Treader* to fulfill his heart's desire: to journey to Aslan's country.

Rhince ✦ The *Dawn Treader's* first mate.

Rynelf ✦ One of the *Dawn Treader's* loyal sailors.

Eustace Clarence Scrubb ✦ Lucy and Edmund's cousin, a nerdy and pompous child whose character is profoundly transformed for the better through his adventures on the *Dawn Treader*. He returns to Narnia in the next adventure, *The Silver Chair*.

99
THE SEVEN LOST LORDS

One of the quests of the Dawn Treader *is to find, or learn the fate of, these men:*

Lord Bern ✦ Appointed Duke of Lone Islands.

Lord Octesian ✦ Fate unknown; presumably died on Dragon Island.

Lord Restimar ✦ Turned into a gold corpse on Deathwater Island.

Lord Rhoop ✦ Rescued from the Dark Island.

Lords Argoz, Mavramorn, and Revilian ✦ The three sleepers at Aslan's Table on Ramandu's Island, cursed to sleep by their quarrel at the feast; only by the *Dawn Treader* traveling to the end of the world and leaving Reepicheep to travel beyond will their curse be lifted.

¶¶¶
OTHER CHARACTERS

The Chief Voice ✦ Head of the Duffers (Island of the Voices).

Clipsie ✦ The Chief Voice's Daughter (Island of the Voices).

Coriakin ✦ A former star, perhaps being punished; governor of the Island of the Voices.

Anne Featherstone ✦ A schoolmate of Lucy's, conjured by a magic spell on the Island of the Voices.

Gumpas ✦ Corrupt Governor of the Lone Islands, removed by King Caspian.

Marjorie Preston ✦ Another of Lucy's schoolmates, conjured by the spell (Island of the Voices).

Pug ✦ Slave-trader on Felimath (Lone Islands).

Ramandu ✦ An aged star, at rest as the guardian of Aslan's Table (Ramandu's Island).

Ramandu's Daughter ✦ Never named by C. S. Lewis, but christened Lilliandil by Douglas Gresham (Lewis's stepson) for the film adaptation of *The Voyage of the Dawn Treader*. The beautiful star-daughter marries King Caspian (Ramandu's Island).

Alberta and Harold Scrubb ✦ Eustace's teetotaling, nonsmoking, vegetarian parents (England).

Jack ✦ Slave dealer on Felimath (Lone Islands).

The Seven Appearances of Aslan

———— ◦—❧⦿❧—◦ ————

Aslan, the noble Lion, son of the Emperor-Over-the-Sea, appears seven times in *The Voyage of the Dawn Treader.*

- ✦ He appears to Eustace on Dragon Island, to help Eustace return to human form.

- ✦ He appears on Deathwater Island when the party is arguing over the magic waters.

- ✦ He appears in the Magician's Book, growling at Lucy when she is tempted to cast the spell for beauty.

- ✦ He appears in Coriakin's house, when Lucy magically summons him.

- ✦ He appears as an albatross to guide the *Dawn Treader* away from the Dark Island.

- ✦ He appears to King Caspian in his cabin after the king tries to abdicate his throne.

- ✦ He appears first as a Lamb, then in his normal form, at the very end of the world.

The Itinerary of the Dawn Treader

After leaving Narnia and picking up the English children, the *Dawn Treader* visits these islands (counting the Lone Islands as one, this means the ship called on seven islands before reaching the very end of the world):

+ **The Lone Islands:** Where slave traders capture several of the crew, but order is restored by King Caspian, who leaves Lord Bern in charge as the Duke of the Lone Islands.

+ **Dragon Island:** The *Dawn Treader* drops anchor here for repairs and rest after sailing through a terrible storm. Here Eustace runs away, is transformed into a dragon, and has a life-changing encounter with Aslan.

+ **The Low Green Island:** Previously inhabited but now deserted, this island is where Reepicheep finds the coracle he will use to sail over the last wave at the end of the world to reach Aslan's country.

+ **Deathwater Island:** Uninhabited island where Lord Restimar met his doom in a well of water that turns to gold anything dipped into it.

+ **The Island of the Voices:** Home of Coriakin and the Duffers/Dufflepuds. Here Lucy performs a magic spell to make hidden things visible (and is rewarded by an encounter with Aslan).

+ **The Dark Island:** The land where dreams (and nightmares) come true. Only by the grace of Aslan does the *Dawn Treader* escape.

✦ **Ramandu's Island:** Site of Aslan's Table, a daily feast for the birds of the dawn (and anyone else who cares to eat). Home of Ramandu and Lilliandil.

✦ **The End of the World:** Upon leaving Ramandu's Island, the ship sails as far as it can, with Reepicheep and the English children venturing further in a rowboat—until finally the Mouse travels on to the very last wave in his coracle. At that point, on a low grassy land, Eustace and his cousins encounter Aslan, who sends them home.

Bibliography

Downing, David C. *Into the Region of Awe: Mysticism in C. S. Lewis.* Downers Grove, IL: InterVarsity Press, 2005.

_____. *Into the Wardrobe: C. S. Lewis and the Narnia Chronicles.* San Francisco: Jossey-Bass, 2005.

Hinten, Marvin D. *The Keys to the Chronicles: Unlocking the Symbols of C. S. Lewis's Narnia.* Nashville: Broadman & Holman, 2005.

Lewis, C. S. *The Collected Letters*, Volume III. San Francisco: HarperSanFrancisco, 2007.

_____. *Letters to Malcolm: Chiefly on Prayer.* San Diego: Harcourt, Inc., 1964.

_____. *The Voyage of the Dawn Treader.* New York: Macmillan Books, 1952.

Ward, Michael. *Planet Narnia: The Seven Heavens in the Imagination of C. S. Lewis.* New York: Oxford University Press, 2008.

About Paraclete Press

Who We Are

Paraclete Press is a publisher of books, recordings, and DVDs on Christian spirituality. Our publishing represents a full expression of Christian belief and practice—from Catholic to Evangelical, from Protestant to Orthodox.

We are the publishing arm of the Community of Jesus, an ecumenical monastic community in the Benedictine tradition. As such, we are uniquely positioned in the marketplace without connection to a large corporation and with informal relationships to many branches and denominations of faith.

What We Are Doing

Books

Paraclete publishes books that show the richness and depth of what it means to be Christian. Although Benedictine spirituality is at the heart of all that we do, we publish books that reflect the Christian experience across many cultures, time periods, and houses of worship. We publish books that nourish the vibrant life of the church and its people—books about spiritual practice, formation, history, ideas, and customs.

We have several different series, including the best-selling Paraclete Essentials and Paraclete Giants series of classic texts in contemporary English; A Voice from the Monastery—men and women monastics writing about living a spiritual life today; award-winning literary faith fiction and poetry; and the Active Prayer Series that brings creativity and liveliness to any life of prayer.

Recordings

From Gregorian chant to contemporary American choral works, our music recordings celebrate sacred choral music through the centuries. Paraclete distributes the recordings of the internationally acclaimed choir Gloriæ Dei Cantores, praised for their "rapt and fathomless spiritual intensity" by *American Record Guide*, and the Gloriæ Dei Cantores Schola, which specializes in the study and performance of Gregorian chant. Paraclete is also the exclusive North American distributor of the recordings of the Monastic Choir of St. Peter's Abbey in Solesmes, France, long considered to be a leading authority on Gregorian chant.

DVDs

Our DVDs offer spiritual help, healing, and biblical guidance for life issues: grief and loss, marriage, forgiveness, anger management, facing death, and spiritual formation.

Learn more about us at our website:
www.paracletepress.com, or call us toll-free at 1-800-451-5006.

More on how to lead the Christian life

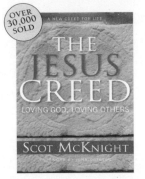

The Jesus Creed
Scot McKnight

ISBN: 978-1-55725-400-9
335 pages, $16.99, Paperback

Scot McKnight gives Christians an opportunity to walk alongside Jesus as he teaches the Jesus Creed—the amended Jewish *Shema*—of love of the Father and love of others.

"For a long time [Scot McKnight] has been a kind of secret weapon for my own education and growth. Now he can be yours as well. This book will bring Jesus' world and yours much closer together."
—JOHN ORTBERG
author of *If You Want to Walk on Water, You've Got to Get Out of the Boat*

Dragon Slayers
Sir Wyvern Pugilist

ISBN: 978-1-55725-779-6
192 pages, $17.99, Oversize paperback

The Christian life requires dragon slaying! Sir Wyvern Pugilist has written a playful new guide for preparing all ages to engage the snarly and slimy monsters presently inhabiting our world. Read for yourself or share with children or grandchildren this playful, enlightening, and informative story in the style of J. R. R. Tolkien.

"Congratulations to Paraclete Press for successfully persuading Sir Wyvern to put pen to paper and for giving us this new manual on Dragon Slaying! It is long overdue! We enthusiastically recommend this guidebook for young and old alike, it's just that good."—Slayers' Weekly

Available from most booksellers or through Paraclete Press:
www.paracletepress.com. 1-800-451-5006. Try your local bookstore first.